PENGUIN BOOKS

RESURRECTION BLUES

ARTHUR MILLER (1915-2005) was born in New York City in 1915 and studied at the University of Michigan. His plays include *All My Sons* (1947), *Death of a Salesman* (1949), *The Crucible* (1953), *A View from the Bridge* and *A Memory of Two Mondays* (1955), *After the Fall* (1964), *Incident at Vichy* (1964), *The Prince* (1968), *The Creation of the World and Other Business* (1972), and *The American Clock*. He as also written a novel, *Focus* (1945), *The Misfits*, which was filmed in 1960, and the text for *In Russia* (1969), *Chinese Encounters* (1979), and *In the Country* (1977), three books of photographs by his wife, Inge Morath. Other works include *Salesman in Beijing* (1984); *Danger: Memory!* (1987); *Timebends*, a memoir (1988); *The Ride Down Mt. Morgan* (1991), *The Last Yankee* (1993); and *Broken Glass* (1994), which won the 1995 Olivier Award for Best Play, and a novella, *Homely Girl, a Life* (1995). Recent plays include *Mr. Peters' Connections*, *Resurrection Blues*, and his last play *Finishing the Picture*. He was awarded the Avery Hopwood Award for Playwrighting at University of Michigan in 1936. He twice won the New York Drama Critics Circle Award, received two Emmy Awards and three Tony Awards for his plays, as well as a Tony Award for Lifetime Achievement. He also won an Obie Award, a BBC Best Play Award, the George Foster Peabody Award, a Gold Medal for Drama from the National Institute of Arts and Letters, the Literary Lion Award from the New York Public Library, the John F. Kennedy Lifetime Achievement Award, and the Algur Meadows Award. He received honorary degrees from Oxford University and Harvard University and was awarded the Prix Moliere of the French theatre, the Dorothy and Lillian Gish Lifetime Achievement Award and the Pulitzer Prize, as well as numerous other awards. He was named the Jefferson Lecturer for the National Endowment for the Humanities in 2001. He was awarded the 2002 Prince of Asturias for Letters and the 2003 Jerusalem Prize.

BY ARTHUR MILLER

DRAMA
The Golden Years
The Man Who Had All the Luck
All My Sons
Death of a Salesman
An Enemy of the People (*adaptation
of the play by Ibsen*)
The Crucible
A View from the Bridge
After the Fall
Incident at Vichy
The Price
The American Clock
The Creation of the World and
Other Business
The Archbishop's Ceiling
The Ride Down Mt. Morgan
Broken Glass
Mr. Peters' Connections
Resurrection Blues

ONE–ACT PLAYS
A View from the Bridge, *one-act
version, with* A Memory of Two
Mondays
Elegy for a Lady (*in* Two-Way
Mirror)
Some Kind of Love Story (*in* Two-
Way Mirror)
I Can't Remember Anything (*in*
Danger: Memory!)
Clara (*in* Danger: Memory!)
The Last Yankee

OTHER WORKS
Situation Normal
The Misfits (*a cinema novel*)
Focus (*a novel*)
I Don't Need You Anymore
(*short stories*)
In the Country (*reportage with Inge
Morath photographs*)
Chinese Encounters (*reportage with
Inge Morath photographs*)
In Russia (*reportage with Inge Morath
photographs*)
Salesman in Beijing (*a memoir*)
Timebends (*autobiography*)
Homely Girl, a Life (*novella*)
On Politics and the Art of Acting

COLLECTIONS
Arthur Miller's Collected Plays
(Volumes I and II)
The Portable Arthur Miller
The Theater Essays of Arthur Miller
(*Robert Martin, editor*)
Echoes Down the Corridor:
Collected Essays, 1944–2000

VIKING CRITICAL LIBRARY
EDITIONS
Death of a Salesman (*edited by
Gerald Weales*)
The Crucible (*edited by
Gerald Weales*)

TELEVISION WORKS
Playing for Time

SCREENPLAYS
The Misfits
Everybody Wins
The Crucible

ARTHUR MILLER

RESURRECTION BLUES

A PROLOGUE AND TWO ACTS

PENGUIN BOOKS

PENGUIN BOOKS

Published by the Penguin Group
Penguin Group (USA) Inc., 375 Hudson Street, New York, New York 10014, U.S.A.
Penguin Group (Canada), 90 Eglinton Avenue East, Suite 700, Toronto,
Ontario, Canada M4P 2Y3 (a division of Pearson Penguin Canada Inc.)
Penguin Books Ltd, 80 Strand, London WC2R 0RL, England
Penguin Ireland, 25 St Stephen's Green, Dublin 2, Ireland (a division of Penguin Books Ltd)
Penguin Group (Australia), 250 Camberwell Road, Camberwell, Victoria 3124, Australia
(a division of Pearson Australia Group Pty Ltd)
Penguin Books India Pvt Ltd, 11 Community Centre, Panchsheel Park,
New Delhi – 110 017, India
Penguin Group (NZ), cnr Airborne and Rosedale Roads, Albany, Auckland 1310,
New Zealand (a division of Pearson New Zealand Ltd)
Penguin Books (South Africa) (Pty) Ltd, 24 Sturdee Avenue, Rosebank,
Johannesburg 2196, South Africa

Penguin Books Ltd, Registered Offices:
80 Strand, London WC2R 0RL, England

First published in Penguin Books 2006

10 9 8 7 6 5 4 3 2 1

LIBRARY OF CONGRESS CATALOGING IN PUBLICATION DATA
Miller, Arthur, 1915–2005
Resurrection blues : a prologue and two acts / Arthur Miller.
p. cm.
ISBN 0 14 30.3548 7
1. Politicians—Drama. 2. Power (Social sciences)—Drama. 3. Women motion picture
producers and directors—Drama. I. Title.
PS3525.I5156R47 2006
812'.52—dc22   2005053506

Printed in the United States of America

A NOTE ABOUT THE PLAY

Resurrection Blues received its world premiere at the Guthrie Theater, Minneapolis, in August 2002 with John Bedford Lloyd as General Felix Barriaux, Jeff Weiss as Henri Schultz, and Laila Robins as Emily Shapiro, directed by David Esbjornson.

CHARACTERS

GENERAL FELIX BARRIAUX, *chief of state*
HENRI SCHULTZ, *his cousin*
EMILY SHAPIRO, *a film director*
SKIP L. CHEESEBORO, *an account executive*
PHIL, *a cameraman*
SARAH, *a soundwoman*
POLICE CAPTAIN
JEANINE, *Schultz's daughter*
STANLEY, *a disciple*

SOLDIERS, WAITERS, PASSERSBY, PEASANTS

PLACE

Various locations in a far away country

RESURRECTION BLUES

PROLOGUE

Dark stage. Light finds Jeanine in wheelchair; she is wrapped in bandages, one leg straight out. She addresses the audience.

JEANINE: Nothing to be alarmed about. I finally decided, one morning, to jump out my window. In this country even a successful suicide is difficult. I seem to be faintly happy that I failed, although god knows why. But of course you can be happy about the strangest things . . . I did not expect failure in my life. I failed as a revolutionary . . . and come to think of it, even as a dope addict—one day the pleasure simply disappeared, along with my husband. We so badly need a revolution here. But that's another story. I refuse to lament. Oddly, in fact, I feel rather cheerful about it all, in a remote way, now that I died, or almost, and have my life again. The pain is something else, but you can't have everything.

Going out the window was a very interesting experience. I can remember passing the third floor on my way down and the glorious sensation of release. Like when I was a student at Barnard and went to Coney Island one Sunday and took that ride on the loop-the-loop and the big drop when you think it won't ever come up again. This time it didn't and I had joined the air, I felt transparent, and I saw so sharply, like a condor, a tiger. I passed our immense jaquaranda tree and there was a young buzzard sitting on a branch, picking his lice. Passing the second floor I saw a cloud over my head the shape of a grand piano. I could almost taste that cloud. Then I saw the cracks in the sidewalk coming up at me and the stick of an Eskimo ice cream bar that had a faint smear of chocolate. And everything I saw seemed superbly precious and for a split second I think I believed in god. Or at least his eye, or *an* eye seeing everything so exactly.

Light finds Henri Schultz.

My father has returned to be of help. I am trying to appreciate his concern after all these years. Like many fools he at times has a certain crazy wisdom. He says now—despite being a philosopher—that I must give up on ideas which only lead to other ideas. Instead I am to think of specific, concrete things. He says the Russians have always had more ideas than any other people in history and ended in the pit. The Americans have no ideas and they have one success after another. I am trying to have no ideas.

Papa is so like our country, a drifting ship heading for where nobody knows—Norway, maybe, or is it Java or Los Angeles? The one thing we know for sure, our treasure that we secretly kiss and adore—is death—

Light finds Emily Shapiro and Skip L. Cheeseboro.

—death and dreams, death and dancing, death and laughter. It is our salt and chile pepper, the flavoring of our lives.

We have eight feet of topsoil here, plenty of rain, we can grow anything, but especially greed. A lot of our people are nearly starving. And a bullet waits for anyone who seriously complains.

Light finds Stanley.

In short—a normal country in this part of the world. A kind of miraculous incompetence, when you look at it.

I had sixteen in my little brigade, including two girls. We were captured. They shot them all in thirty seconds.

Light finds Felix Barriaux.

My uncle Felix, the head of the country, spared me. I still find it hard to forgive him. I think it is one of the contradictions that sent me out my window. Survival can be hard to live with. . . . None of my people was over nineteen.

Light finds nothing.

I have a friend now. When I woke on the sidewalk he was lying beside me in my blood, embracing me and howling like a child in pain. He saved me. His love. He comes some nights and brings me honor for having fought.

The last light brightens.

Up in the mountains the people think he is the son of god. Neither of us is entirely sure of that. I suppose we'll have to wait and see.

Brightens further still. Slight pause.

What will happen now, will happen: I am content.

> *She rolls into darkness. The last light brightens even further, widening its reach until it fully covers the stage.*

SCENE I

*Office of the Chief of State, Felix Barriaux. He is
seated at a window near his desk, studying a letter
while filing his nails. Intercom barks.*

FELIX, *To intercom:* My cousin? Yes, but didn't he say this afternoon? Well, ask him in. . . . Wait. *Tension as he studies the
letter again.* All right, but interrupt me in fifteen minutes; he
can go on and on. You know these intellectuals. —Anything
in the afternoon papers? The radio? And the Miami station?
Good. . . . Listen, Isabelle . . . are you alone? —I want you to
forget last night, agreed? Exactly, and we will, we'll try again
soon. I appreciate your understanding, my dear, you're a fantastic girl . . .

You can send in Mr. Schultz. *In conflict he restudies the letter,
then* . . . Oh, fuck all intellectuals! *He passionately, defiantly
kisses the letter and stashes it in his inside pocket.*

Henri enters. Wears a cotton jacket and a tweed cap.

Henri! Welcome home! Wonderful to see you; and you look
so well!

HENRI, *solemn smile:* Felix.

FELIX, *both hands smothering Henri's:* —I understood you to say this afternoon.

HENRI, *confused:* Did I? *Touching his forehead* . . . Well I suppose I could come back if you're . . .

FELIX: Out of the question! Sit! Please! *Shaking his head, amazed—before Henri can sit.* I can't help it.

HENRI: What?

FELIX: I look at you, cousin, and I see the best years of our lives.

HENRI, *embarrassed:* Yes, I suppose.

Now they sit.

FELIX: You don't agree.

HENRI: I have too much on my mind to think about it.

FELIX, *grinning feigns shooting with pistol at Henri:* . . . You sound like you're bringing me trouble . . . I hope not.

HENRI: The contrary, Felix, I'd like to keep you out of trouble . . .

FELIX: What does that mean?

HENRI: I didn't want to take up your office time, but there was no answer at your house . . . have you moved?

FELIX: No, but . . . I sleep in different places every night. —
No guarantee, but I try to make it a little harder for them.

HENRI: Then the war is still on? I see hardly anything in the
European press . . .

FELIX: Well, it's hardly a war anymore; comes and goes now,
like a mild diarrhea. What is it, two years?

HENRI: More like three, I think.

FELIX: No. There was still major fighting three years ago. You
came afterward.

HENRI: That's right, isn't it. —God, my mind is gone.

FELIX: Listen, I lied to you—you're not looking good at all.
Wait! —I have some new vitamins! *Presses intercom.* Isabelle!
Give my cousin a bottle of my new vitamins when he leaves.
To Henri: French.

HENRI: What?

FELIX: My vitamins are French.

HENRI: Your vitamins are French?

FELIX: —What's the matter?

HENRI: I'm . . . very troubled, Felix.

FELIX: Jeanine.

HENRI: Partly. . . . It's that . . . at times nothing seems to follow from anything else.

FELIX: Oh, well, I wouldn't worry about a thing like that.

HENRI: I've always envied how you accept life, Felix.

FELIX: Maybe you read too many books—life is complicated, but underneath the principle has never changed since the Romans—fuck them before they can fuck you. How's Jeanine now?

HENRI: What can I say? —I'm with her every day and there are signs that she wants to live . . . but who knows? The whole thing is a catastrophe.

FELIX: I know her opinion of me, but I still think that girl has a noble heart; she's a Greek tragedy. . . . You remember my son-in-law, the accountant? He calculates that falling from the third floor— *Raises his arm straight up.* —she must have hit the sidewalk at sixty-two miles an hour. *Slaps his hand loudly on desktop.*

HENRI, *pained:* Please.

FELIX: But at least it brought you together. Sorry. Incidentally, where's your dentist?

HENRI: My dentist?

FELIX: I am practically commuting to Miami but my teeth keep falling apart. Where do you go?

HENRI: It depends. New York, London, Paris . . . wherever I happen to be. Listen, Felix . . . *Breaks off.* I don't know where to begin . . .

FELIX: . . . I hope it's not some kind of problem for me because I'll be frank with you, Henri—I'm not . . . completely myself these days. —I'm all right, you understand, but I'm just . . . not myself.

HENRI: . . . I didn't come to antagonize you.

FELIX, *in a flare of anger-alarm*: How the hell could you antagonize me! I love you, you bastard. . . . Tell me, you still living in New York?

HENRI: Mostly Munich. Lecturing on Tragedy.

FELIX: Tragedy is my life, Henri—when I was training in Georgia those Army dentists were the best, but I didn't have a cavity then. Now, when I'm paying the bills I'm full of holes. —How do you lecture on Tragedy?

HENRI, *inhales, exhales:* Let me tell you what's on my . . .

FELIX, *now a certain anxiety begins to seep out more openly:* Yes! Go ahead, what is it? . . . Isn't that cap too hot?

HENRI: It helps my arthritis.

FELIX: Oh, right! And how does that work again? —Oh yes!—it's that most of the body heat escapes through the skull . . .

HENRI: Exactly . . .

FELIX, *suddenly recalling:* . . . So it keeps your joints warm!—this is why I always loved talking to you, Henri!—you make my mind wander. . . . Wait! My god, I haven't congratulated you; your new wife.

HENRI: Thank you.

FELIX: I read that she's a concert pianist?

HENRI, *a strained smile:* . . . You're going to have to hear this, Felix.

FELIX: I'm listening! —But seeing you again always . . . moves me. *Reaches over to touch Henri's knee.* I am moved. *Collects himself.* How long will you be staying this time?

HENRI: A month or two; depends on how Jeanine progresses . . .

FELIX: Doctor Herman tells me she'll need another operation.

HENRI: Two more, possibly three. The whole thing is devastating.

FELIX: . . . I have to say, I never thought you were this close . . .

HENRI: No one can be close to a drug addict; but she's absolutely finished with that now. I was never much of a father but I'm going to see her back to health if it's the last thing I ever do.

FELIX: Bravo, I'm glad to hear that. —How a woman of her caliber could go for drugs is beyond me. What happened, do you know?

HENRI, *sudden surge:* What happened!—she lost a revolution, Felix.

FELIX: All right, but she has to know all that is finished, revolution is out . . . I'm talking everywhere.

HENRI: . . . Listen, don't make me drag it out—I haven't the strength.

FELIX: Yes. Please. —But I must tell you, it always amazes me how you gave up everything to just read books and *think.* Frankly, I have never understood it. But go ahead . . .

HENRI: Day before yesterday I drove with my wife up toward Santa Felice to show her the country.

FELIX: According to this *Vanity Fair* magazine that is one of the finest views in the world, you know.

HENRI: As we were passing through the villages . . .

FELIX: . . . Also the *National Geographic.*

HENRI: When we got up there, Felix . . . it all came back to me . . . remember when we were students and hiked up there together? Remember our shock and disgust that so many of the children had orange hair . . .

FELIX, *a happy memory; laughs indulgently:* Ah yes! The blood fluke . . . it's in the water. But it's practically harmless, you know.

HENRI: Not for children. It can destroy a child's liver . . .

FELIX: Well now, that's a bit . . .

HENRI, *sudden sharpness:* It is true, Felix! And the symptom of course is orange hair.

FELIX: What's your point?

HENRI: What's my point! Felix, blood fluke in the water supply in the twenty-first century is. . . . My god, you are the head of this country, don't you feel a . . . ?

FELIX: They won't boil the water, what can I do about it! — What is all this about the fluke suddenly? The British are definitely going to build a gigantic warehouse on the harbor, for god's sake!

HENRI, *distressed:* A warehouse! What's that got to do with . . .

FELIX: Because this country's starting to move and you're still talking blood fluke! I assure you, Henri, nobody in this country has the slightest interest in blood fluke!—Is this what you wanted to talk to me about?

HENRI: You probably won't remember, but on my last visit I brought home an eighteenth-century painting from Paris, cost me twenty-six thousand dollars. The pollution in our air has since peeled off about a third of the paint.

FELIX: That couldn't happen in Paris?

HENRI: It's been sitting in Paris for two hundred and fifty years! . . . I had a grand piano shipped from New York for my wife . . .

FELIX: The varnish cracked?

HENRI: The varnish did not crack but my architect is afraid the floor may collapse because of the underground leakage of water from the aqueduct, which has undermined the foundations of that whole lovely neighborhood. And brought in termites!

FELIX: I'm to chase termites?

HENRI: —My wife has to practice in the garage, Felix! When she plays for me I have to sit listening in the Mercedes!

FELIX: But cousin, a grand piano—you're talking three-quarters of a ton!

HENRI: I was getting out of a taxi yesterday on Avenue Fontana, our number-one shopping street . . .

FELIX: Did you see the new Dunhill store . . . ?

HENRI: . . . I nearly stepped on a dead baby lying at the curb.

Felix throws up his hands and walks away, steaming.

Shoppers were passing by, saw it, and walked on. As I did.

FELIX: What is all this suddenly? None of this has ever been any different!

HENRI: I don't know! I suppose I never really *looked* at anything. It may be Jeanine; she was so utterly beautiful, Felix.

FELIX: Oh god, yes.

HENRI: I think I never really *saw* what I meant to her. Sitting with her day after day now . . . for the first time I understood my part in her suffering. I betrayed her, Felix. It's terrible.

FELIX: Why? You always gave her everything . . .

HENRI: A faith in the revolution is what I gave her . . . and then walked away from it myself.

FELIX: I hope I'm not hearing your old Marxism again . . .

HENRI: Oh shit, Felix!—I haven't been a Marxist for twenty-five years!

FELIX: Because that is finished, they're almost all in narcotics now, thanks be to god; but the Americans are here now and they'll clean out the whole lot of them by New Years! Your guerillas are done!

HENRI: These are not my guerillas, my guerillas were foolish, idealistic people, but the hope of the world! These people now are cynical and stupid enough to deal narcotics!

FELIX: Listen, after thirty-eight years of civil war what did you expect to find here, Sweden? Weren't you in analysis once?

HENRI: Yes. I was. Twenty years ago at least. Why?

FELIX: I'm seeing a man in Miami.

HENRI: Well, that's surprising. I always think of you in control of everything.

FELIX: Not the most important thing.

HENRI: . . . You don't say. Maybe you have the wrong woman.

FELIX: They can't all be wrong. My dog just won't hunt.

HENRI: Imagine. And analysis helps?

FELIX, *hesitates:* Semi. I'm trying to keep from letting it obsess me. But I have this vision, you know?

HENRI: Oh? Someone you've met?

FELIX: No, just imaginary—like those women you see in New York. Tall, you know? Fine teeth. Kind of . . . I don't know . . . nasty. Or spirited . . . spirited is the word. Is your wife tall?

HENRI: No. She's Viennese. Rather on the short, round side.

FELIX: I've tried short and round, but . . . *Shakes his head.* It's torturing me, Henri. Listen, how would you like to be ambassador to Moscow again?

HENRI, *gripping his head:* Do you see why I am depressed?— nothing follows!

FELIX: —The reason you're depressed is . . .

HENRI, *grips his head:* I beg you, Felix, don't tell me why I'm depressed!

FELIX: . . . It's because you're a rich man in a poor country, that's all . . . but we're moving, by god!

Intercom. Felix bends to it.

Thank you, my dear. *To Henri:* —I have a meeting. . . . What'd you want to tell me?

HENRI, *a pause to organize:* On our little trip to Santa Felice— Hilda and I—we were struck by a . . . what to call it? . . . a kind of spiritual phenomenon up there. Really incredible. Wherever we went the peasants had pictures of this young man whom they . . .

FELIX: He's finished. We've captured him, Henri, he is history, all done.

HENRI: They keep candles lit before his photograph, you know . . . like a saint.

FELIX: This saint's gunmen have shot up three police stations and killed two officers and wounded five more in the past two months.

HENRI: They say he personally had nothing to do with the violence.

FELIX: The man is a revolutionary and he is responsible! — Listen, Henri, two of my brothers died fighting shits like these and he will have no mercy from me. Is this what you wanted to talk to about?

HENRI: There is a rumor—which I find hard to believe—that you intend to crucify this fellow?

FELIX: I can't comment on that.

HENRI: Beg your pardon?

FELIX: No comment, Henri, that's the end of it.

HENRI: And if this brings on a bloodbath?

FELIX: Don't think it will.

HENRI: Felix, you are totally out of touch. They really think he is the Messiah, the son of god!

FELIX: The son of god is a man named Ralph?

HENRI: But a crucifixion! Don't you see?—it will prove they were right! These are simple people, it could bring them roaring down out of the mountains!

FELIX: Shooting doesn't work! People are shot on television every ten minutes; bang-bang, and they go down like dolls, it's meaningless. But nail up a couple of these bastards, and believe me this will be the quietest country on the continent and ready for development! A crucifixion always quiets things down. Really, I am amazed—a cretin goes about preaching bloody revolution, and you . . .

HENRI: Talk to the people! They'll tell you he's preaching justice.

FELIX: Oh come off it, Henri! Two percent of our people— including you—own ninety-six percent of the land. The justice they're demanding is your land; are you ready to give it to them?

HENRI: . . . To tell the truth, yes, I just might be. I returned to try to help Jeanine but also . . . I've decided to put the business and both farms up for sale.

FELIX: Why!—those farms are terrific!

HENRI: They've been raising coca and it's impossible to police my managers when I'm away so much; in short, I've decided to stop pretending to be a business man . . . *Breaks off*.

FELIX: Really. And what's stopping you?

HENRI: Courage, probably. I lack enough conviction . . .

FELIX: No, Henri, it's your common sense telling you that in ten years the land you gave away will end up back in the hands of two percent of the smartest people! You can't teach a baboon to play Chopin. —Or are you telling me this idiot is the son of god?

HENRI: I don't believe in god, let alone his son. I beg you, Felix, listen to what I'm saying . . . you crucify this fellow and our country is finished, ruined!

FELIX: Henri, dear friend . . . *Draws the letter out of his jacket pocket.* . . . not only are we not ruined—I can tell you that with this crucifixion our country will finally begin to live!

This fax arrived this morning.

A gigantic fax unspurls.

You've heard of Thomson, Weber, Macdean and Abramowitz of Madison Avenue?

HENRI: Of course . . . Thomson, Weber, Macdean and Abramowitz. They're the largest advertising agency for pharmaceutical companies.

FELIX: So I'm told. How they got wind of it I don't know, unless General Gonzalez contacted them for a finder's fee—he's our consul in New York now; anyway, they want to photograph the crucifixion for television.

HENRI: What in god's name are you talking about?

FELIX, *hands the letter to Henri:* This is an offer of seventy-five million dollars for the exclusive worldwide rights to televise the crucifixion.

HENRI, *stunned, he reads the letter:* Have you read these conditions?

FELIX: What do you mean?

HENRI, *indicating letter:* They will attach commercial announcements!

FELIX: But they say "dignified" announcements. . . . Probably like the phone company or, I don't know, the Red Cross.

HENRI: They are talking underarm deodorants, Felix!

FELIX: You don't know that!

HENRI, *slapping the letter:* Read it! They hardly expect a worldwide audience for the phone company! They're talking athlete's foot, Felix!

FELIX: Oh no, I don't think they . . .

HENRI: They're talking athlete's foot, sour stomach, constipation, anal itch . . . !

FELIX: No-no!

HENRI: Where else does seventy-five million come from? I'm sure they figure it would take him four or five hours to die, so they could load it up—runny stool, falling hair, gum disease, crotch itch, dry skin, oily skin, nasal blockage, diapers for grownups . . . impotence . . .

FELIX: God no, they'd never do that!

HENRI: Why not? Is there a hole in the human anatomy we don't make a dollar on? With a crucifixion the sky's the limit! I forgot ear wax, red eyes, bad breath . . .

FELIX: Please, Henri, sit down for a moment.

HENRI, *sitting:* It's a catastrophe! And for me personally it's . . . it's the end!

FELIX: Why?—nobody will blame you . . .

HENRI: My company distributes most of those products, for god's sake!

FELIX: I think maybe you're exaggerating the reaction . . .

HENRI: Am I! As your men drive nails into his hands and split the bones of his feet the camera will cut away to . . . god knows what . . . somebody squirming with a burning ass-hole! You must let the fellow go . . . !

FELIX: He's not going anywhere, he's a revolutionary and an idiot!

HENRI: You're not visualizing, Felix! People are desperate for someone this side of the stars who feels their suffering him-self and gives a damn! The man is hope!

FELIX: He is hope because he gets us seventy-five million! My god, we once had an estimate to irrigate the entire eastern half of the country and that was only thirteen million! This is fantastic!

HENRI: Felix—if you sell this man, you will join the two other most contemptible monsters in history.

FELIX: What two others?

HENRI: Pontius Pilate and Judas, for god's sake! That kind of infamy is very hard to shed.

FELIX: Except that Jesus Christ was not an impostor and this one is.

HENRI: We don't know that.

FELIX: What the hell are you talking about, the son of a bitch is not even Jewish!—Good god, Henri, with that kind of money I could put the police into decent shoes and issue every one of them a poncho. And real sewers . . . with *pipes!*—so the better class of people wouldn't have to go up to the tops of the hills to build a house . . . we could maybe have our own airline and send all our prostitutes to the dentist . . .

HENRI: Stop. Please. *Slight pause.* Do you really want our country blamed for a worldwide suicide?

FELIX: *What?*

HENRI: A crucifixion lasting possibly hours on the screen— use your imagination! To a lot of people it will mean the imminent end of the world . . .

FELIX, *dismissing:* Oh that's nonsense . . . !

HENRI: I can see thousands jumping off bridges in Paris, London, New York . . . ! And California . . . my god, California will turn into a madhouse. —*And the whole thing blamed on us?* —*We'll be a contemptible country!* I know you'll call it off now, won't you.

Felix stares.

Felix, think of your children—their father will be despised through the end of time, do you want that stain on their lives?

Pause. Felix in thought.

FELIX: I disagree. I really do. Look at it calmly—fifteen or twenty years after they kicked Nixon out of the White House he had one of the biggest funerals since Abraham Lincoln. Is that true or isn't it?

HENRI: Well, yes, I suppose it is.

FELIX: Believe me, Henri, in politics there is only one sacred rule—nobody clearly remembers anything.

HENRI: I've seen him.

FELIX: Really! How'd that happen?

HENRI: The police happened to have caught him in the street outside my window. Terrible scene; four or five of his . . . I suppose you could call them disciples stood there, weeping.

One of the cops clubbed him down and kicked him squarely in the mouth. I was paralyzed. But then, as they were pushing him into the van—quite accidentally, his gaze rose up to my window and for an instant our eyes met. —His composure, Felix—his poise—there was a kind of tranquility in his eyes that was . . . chilling; he almost seemed to transcend everything, as though he knew all this had to happen . . .

FELIX: I thank you for this conversation, it's cleared me up . . .

HENRI: Let me talk to him. I take it you have him here?

FELIX: He won't open his mouth.

HENRI: Let me try to convince him to leave the country.

FELIX: Wonderful, but try to feel out if we can expect some dignity if he's nailed up? I don't want it to look like some kind of torture or something . . .

HENRI: And what about our dignity!

FELIX: Our dignity is modernization! Tell him he's going to die for all of us!

HENRI: . . . Because we need that money!

FELIX: All right, yes, but that's a hell of a lot better than dying for nothing!

> *Felix opens the door; a blinding white light pours through the doorway through which they are peering.*

HENRI: What is that light on him?

FELIX: Nothing. He just suddenly lights up sometimes. It happens, that's all.

HENRI: It "happens"!

FELIX, *defensive outburst:* All right, I don't understand it! Do you understand a computer chip? Can you tell me what electricity is? And how about a gene? I mean what is a fucking gene? So he lights up; it's one more *thing,* that's all. But look at him, you ever seen such total vacancy in a man's face? *Pointing.* That idiot is mental and he's making us all crazy! Go and godspeed!

HENRI, *takes a step toward doorway and halts:* You know, when I saw him outside my window a very odd thought . . . exploded in my head—that I hadn't actually been *seeing* anything . . . for most of my life. That I have lived half blind . . . to Jeanine, even to my former wife . . . I can't begin to explain it, Felix, but it's all left me with one idea that I can't shake off—it haunts me.

FELIX: What idea?

HENRI: That I could have loved. *Slight pause.* In my life.

> *Henri, conflicted, exits through the doorway. Felix shuts the door behind him.*

FELIX: Odd—one minute I'd really love to blow that moron away. But the next minute . . .

*He stares in puzzlement. He goes to his phone. Picks
up the letter.*

Isabelle. Get me New York. 212-779-8865. Want to speak to a
Mr. . . . *Reads letter.* Skip L. Cheeseboro, he's a vice president
of the firm. —Well, yes—if they ask you, say it's in reference
to a crucifixion. He'll know what it means.

Blackout.

SCENE 2

Mountain top. Emily Shapiro enters with Skip L. Cheeseboro. She is in jeans and zipper jacket and baseball cap, he in bush jacket, carrying a portfolio and a shooting stick. They bend over to catch their breaths. Now she straightens up and looks out front, awed.

EMILY: My god! Look at this!

SKIP: Yeah!

EMILY: That snow. That sun. That light!

SKIP: Yeah!

EMILY: What a blue! What an orange! What mountains!

SKIP: What's the date today?

EMILY: Seventeenth.

SKIP: Huh! . . . I think she's getting the divorce today and I completely forgot to call her.

EMILY: Well maybe she'll forgive you. *Looking into distance.* — This is absolutely awesome. How pure.

SKIP: A lot like Nepal—the Ivory Soap shoot.

EMILY: Like Kenya too, maybe . . . Chevy Malibu.

SKIP: The Caucasus, too.

EMILY: Caucasus?

SKIP: Head and Shoulders.

EMILY: Wasn't that Venezuela?

SKIP: Venezuela was Jeep.

EMILY: Right! —No! —Jeep was the Himalayas.

SKIP: Himalayas was Alka Seltzer, dear.

EMILY: Oh right, that gorgeous bubbling fountain.

SKIP: I think the bubbling fountain was Efferdent in Chile.

EMILY, *closing her eyes in anguish:* God, what a mush it all is! *Looking out again.* Human beings don't deserve this world. *Spreading out her arms.* I mean look at this! Look at this glory! . . . And look at us.

The Captain enters.

CAPTAIN: Everything is fine?

SKIP: Beautiful, thank you very much, Captain. Our crew will be arriving shortly . . .

CAPTAIN: We will help them up . . .

Important news.

Mr. Schultz is already arriving.

EMILY: Mr. Schultz?

CAPTAIN: Very famous; his company is making the medicine for the feet.

EMILY AND SKIP, *uncomprehending:* Ah!

EMILY: Oh!—athlete's foot!

CAPTAIN: And for the ears . . . to remove the wax.

SKIP: Really. And what connection does he have with . . . ?

CAPTAIN: He is cousin to General Barriaux . . . very important. *A wide gesture front.* This is the perfect scenery, no?—for the crucifixion?

EMILY, *laughs:* For the what?

SKIP: Thank you, Captain . . .

CAPTAIN: Yes! I must go down; I am speaking English?

SKIP: Oh yes, you speak very well.

CAPTAIN: How you say "lunch"?

SKIP: Lunch? Well . . . lunch.

CAPTAIN: We also. You say lunch and we say lunch.

EMILY: That's really remarkable.

CAPTAIN, *pleased with himself:* Thank you, Madame.

He leaves.

EMILY: That wonderful?—a great spot for a crucifixion!

SKIP, *empty laugh:* Yes . . . Darling, what exactly did Atcheson tell you?

Captain reenters with Henri.

CAPTAIN: Ah, here is Mr. Schultz!! *To Henri:* Here is our director!

HENRI, *to Emily and Skip:* How do you do?

CAPTAIN: I am honored, sir. My wife and daughter are taking "Schultz's" every month!

HENRI, *trying to get back to Emily:* . . . Thank you, but I have very little to do with the company anymore.

CAPTAIN: You also have very good pills for the malaria.

HENRI, *turning to Skip:* I am Henri Schultz . . .

EMILY: Emily Shapiro. Director. This is my producer, Mr. Cheeseboro. We're making a commercial up here.

HENRI: So I understand. I believe the General will be coming up; I have something I'd like to say to you both if you have a moment . . .

EMILY: We're just laying out possible backgrounds . . . *Turning to Skip.* . . . Although I still haven't been told what exactly we're shooting . . .

SKIP: . . . May I ask your involvement, sir? Or should I know?

HENRI: Well let me see—my involvement, I suppose, is my concern for the public peace or something in that line.

SKIP: I don't understand. —If you mean good taste, Miss Shapiro has given the world some of its most uplifting commercial images. And luckily, the beauty of this location practically cries out for a . . . ah . . .

HENRI: A crucifixion, yes. But if you can give me five minutes, I'd like to speak to you about . . .

EMILY: What is he talking about?

SKIP, *to Henri, walking her away:* Excuse us, please. *To Emily*: What exactly did Atcheson tell you?

EMILY: Practically nothing. —Phoned from his limo and said to get my crew right over to Kennedy and the company jet and you'd fill me in when I got here . . .

SKIP: That's all?

EMILY: Wait a minute—yes; he sort of mentioned some kind of execution, but I didn't get the product . . . —What is it, somebody making an execution movie, is that it? And I grab some footage?

HENRI: Candidly, I wouldn't rule out a certain danger . . .

SKIP: There is no danger whatsoever; they have troops all over the mountain.

CAPTAIN: . . . Everything is absolutely covered.

EMILY: Why?

SKIP: Well, let's see. There is this sort of revolutionary terrorist.

EMILY: *Terrorist?* A real one?

HENRI: Actually, he himself is apparently not a . . .

SKIP: The man is totally vicious! His gang have killed some cops and blown up government buildings. And he goes around claiming to be the . . . like, you know, the son of god. *Turning on Henri nervously.* —Is there something I can help you with, sir . . . I mean, what is it you want?

EMILY: I'm confused—what's the product? *To Henri:* What are all those soldiers doing down below?

SKIP: They always have soldiers . . . even around weddings . . . rock concerts . . . anything.

HENRI: This is a bit different, they are there in case of a protest.

EMILY: Protest about what?

SKIP: Sir? We are here under an agreement with General Barriaux, and you are interfering with our work; I'm afraid I really must ask you to leave . . .

> Soldiers enter, dark local men; two carry spades, and a long beam which they set down. One carries a submachine gun and a chainsaw—he stands guard.

EMILY: What's this now?

SKIP: They're putting up a little set. *To the soldiers:* Very good, gentlemen, but don't do anything yet, okay? Just sit down and wait a few minutes, okay? We'll be with you in a few seconds, okay?

> The soldiers nod agreeably but begin unpacking tools— an electric drill, bolts. One of them lays a beam across another.

HENRI: You know it's to be a crucifixion?—

EMILY: A crucifixion. Really. But what's the product? *Calling to the soldiers:* Wait gentlemen! Don't do anything till I tell you, okay?

*The soldiers nod agreeably and one of them begins
digging a hole. Skip grasps the shovel handle.*

No, wait, fellas; for one thing, I've got to decide on the
camera angle before you build anything, okay?

The guard shifts his gun nervously.

Oh well, go ahead.

*They proceed with the digging as she turns to Skip
with beginning alarm.*

Will you kindly explain what the hell is going on here? And
what am I shooting, please?

SKIP: . . . It's a common thing with murderers here . . . they
attach the prisoner . . .

EMILY: Attach? What do you mean? To what?

A very short burst from an electrical drill interrupts.

Please stop that!

*Drill cuts out and in the momentary silence the
Captain, to Henri . . .*

CAPTAIN, *patting his own stomach:* Also you have the best for
the gas . . . "Schultz's"!

HENRI: Captain, please—I inherited the company but I have very little to do with running it. I am a philosopher, a teacher . . .

SKIP: Darling, you must understand—this fellow has blown up a number of *actual* buildings, so they're quite angry with him . . .

EMILY: Wait, Skip—I don't know where I got the idea but I thought somebody was shooting a movie and we were just hitchhiking onto it . . .

SKIP: There's no movie.

EMILY: So . . . is that a cross?

SKIP: Well . . . *Takes a fortifying breath.* In effect.

EMILY: It's really a *crucifixion*?

SKIP: Well . . . in effect, yes, it's very common here . . .

EMILY: "In effect"—you mean like with nails?

HENRI: That's correct.

SKIP: It is not! I was told they'll most likely just tie him onto it! *To Emily:* They do that quite a lot in this country. I mean with death sentences.

EMILY: But he's not actually going to like . . . die . . .

SKIP, *frustration exploding:* I cannot believe that Atcheson . . . !

EMILY: Atcheson told me to get here, period! He didn't say "die"! Nobody dies in a commercial! Have you all gone crazy?

SKIP: We're only photographing it, we're not *doing* it, for god's sake!

EMILY, *clapping hands over ears:* Please stop talking!

> *A soldier starts up a chainsaw. She rushes to him,*
> *waving her arms.*

Prego, Signor . . . No, that's Italian. Bitte . . . not bitte . . . stop, okay? What's Spanish for "stop"?

HENRI: Stop.

EMILY: Yes. *To the men:* Stop!

> *They stop.*

Gracias. Muchos. *To Skip:* I'm sorry, Skip—I think maybe I'm just out.

SKIP: Now you stop being silly!

CAPTAIN: This is going to be a very good thing, Madame. It will frighten the people, you see.

EMILY: And that's good?

CAPTAIN: Oh yes . . . it's when they are not frightened of the government is when they get in trouble. Of course, it would be even better if they were allowed to say whatever they want. Like in the States.

HENRI: Well that's a surprise, coming from the police.

CAPTAIN: Oh, but is a very simple thing—if the troublemakers are allowed to speak they are much easier to catch.

His handheld intercom erupts. He holds it to his ear.

The General has arrived!

Captain rushes out.

HENRI: You may start a bloodbath in this country, sir, I hope you realize that.

SKIP: You are endangering this woman's career! *To Emily:* This could move you into a whole new area. I mean just for starters, if you shot him against the view of those incredible mountains . . .

EMILY: You mean on the cross?

SKIP: Emily dear, you know I adore you. Have I ever steered you wrong? This is a door to possibly Hollywood. There's never been anything remotely like this in the history of television.

EMILY: —And when are we talking about? For it to happen? Just out of curiosity.

SKIP: Toward sundown would be best, but it has to be today.

EMILY: Why?

SKIP: . . . Well, basically . . .

EMILY: Don't tell me "basically," just tell me why.

SKIP: Well, basically because the story is bound to jump the border and we'll have CNN here and ABC and every goddam camera in Europe. So it has to be done today because we have an exclusive.

HENRI: I beg you both, let us discuss this rationally.

EMILY: My head is spinning.

SKIP: I share your feelings, believe me, but . . .

EMILY: . . . I mean there's something deeply, deeply offensive, Skip.

HENRI: That's the point precisely.

EMILY: Really. I think it like . . . disgusts me. Doesn't it you?

SKIP: In a way, I suppose, but realistically, who am I to be disgusted? I mean . . .

> *Suddenly, the gigantic cross is raised, dominating the stage. Emily, struck, raises her hand to silence Skip, who turns to look as it rises to position while soldiers observe to figure if it is the right height.*

All right, dear, let's parse this out head-on, okay? *She is staring into space now, into herself. Sudden new idea.* Showing it on the world screen could help put an end to it forever! *Warming.* Yes! That's it! If I were moralistic I'd even say you have a *duty* to shoot this! Really. I mean that.

> *Soldiers take down the pole and start up a chainsaw again, which stops their talk. The pole is sawed shorter.*

In fact, it could end up a worldwide blow against capital punishment, which I know you are against as I passionately am. Please, dear, come here . . .

> *She doesn't move.*

Darling, please!

> *He goes upstage of the soldiers and the beams. Half in a dream she reluctantly joins him and he holds arms out.*

Look at this!—if you shot from here, with that sky and the mountains . . .

EMILY: But, Skip, I've never in my life shot anything like . . . real—I do commercials!

SKIP: But your genius is that everything you shoot *becomes* real, darling—

EMILY: My genius is to make everything comfortably fake, Skip. No agency wants real. You want a fake-looking crucifixion?—call me.

SKIP: Dear, what you do is make real things look fake, and that makes them emotionally real, whereas . . .

EMILY: Stop. Just stop it, Skip. Please. I'm totally lost. All I know is that somebody actually dying in my lens would melt my eyeball. —I have to call New York . . .

She takes out cell phone.

SKIP: No, dear, please . . .

EMILY: I can't call my mother?

SKIP: Your mother! —Of course. *Handing her his cell phone.* Use mine, charge it to us. And darling, please don't feel . . .

EMILY, *punching the numbers, yells, outraged, scared:* Skip, I beg you do not use ordinary beseeching language to me, okay?! This is death we're talking about!

She dials.

SKIP, *suddenly turning on Henri:* Sir, I appreciate who you are, but if you refuse to leave I will be forced to call the police!

HENRI: Sir, my family has been in this country since the Conquistadors.

SKIP: Really. Conquistadors named Schultz?

HENRI: Cortez had a German doctor.

SKIP, *one-upped, growing desperate:* You don't say!

EMILY, *in phone:* Mother! Yes! Hello? *To Skip:* Now listen, I haven't agreed to anything, okay? —Hello?

> *Captain enters, glancing about; Emily mouths a conversation into the phone.*

CAPTAIN: My excuses, please! General Barriaux is approaching below. I am to ask if there are any firearms . . . pistols, long knives, please to hand them to me. I am speaking English.

HENRI: Don't bother, Captain . . . I'm sure they're not armed.

CAPTAIN, *salutes:* Very good, sir! From Mister Schultz I accept this reassurance! You know, since I was a little child . . . when I was coughing . . . my mother always gave me . . .

HENRI: Will you stop that? Just stop it. This is a serious event, Captain!

> *Skip settles onto his shooting stick, takes out a magazine and affects to blithely work a crossword puzzle.*

EMILY, *in phone:* . . . Mother, please! Listen a minute, will you? . . . It is, yes, it's beautiful. And the birds, yes, they're sensational. I saw a condor, twelve-foot wingspread, unbelievable, it can carry off a goat! —Listen, I left in such a hurry I forgot my cleaning woman doesn't come today so could you go over and feed my cats? Thanks, dear, but just the one can for both, I mean don't have pity, okay? What?

SKIP, *to Henri:* Sir, we are trying to work here . . . I'd be happy to meet somewhere later . . . tomorrow, perhaps . . .

EMILY, *in phone:* —Do I? Well I am nervous, they've just thrown a whole pail of garbage at me and I don't know what to do with it. Well it turns out it's a . . . well, a crucifixion. Some kind of Communist, I suppose. Not as far as I know— *Louder.* I said he's not Jewish as far as I know!

SKIP, *glancing up from his puzzle:* But she mustn't mention . . .

EMILY: But you mustn't mention this to anybody, you understand? —Of course it's a problem for me! I'd be on the next plane but I just signed for my new apartment and I was depending totally on this check.

SKIP: You'll have walked twice in one year, darling—case closed.

EMILY: This'd be my second time I walked off a shoot . . . well the slaughter of the baby seals last year. So I'm a little scared. —And it's also that I'm a little late. —Well, who wouldn't be edgy! I mean I don't know, do I want it or don't I? —Well . . . to tell you the truth I'm not sure, it could have been Max Fleisher. —What marry? —I should marry Max Fleisher? I'm not sure it was him anyway. —Mother, please will you listen, dear; I have no interest in marrying anybody. —I profoundly don't know why! Except I can't imagine being with the same person the entire rest of my life. —But I do believe in people—it's just myself I have doubts about.

The crew enters: Phil, cameraman; Sarah, soundwoman.

Got to run, don't forget the cats and give Daddy a kiss for me. I'll call tomorrow. 'Bye!

PHIL, *sets camera on the ground:* Skip. Good morning, director, what are we shooting?

SARAH: Emily, please could I use your cell phone, I've got to call New York.

EMILY: Is it all right, Skip?

SKIP: Why can't you call from the hotel?

SARAH: Because it's just after nine and they said I could get my pregnancy report after nine and I can't wait.

EMILY: Sarah, really! Isn't that fantastic!

SARAH, *jumping up and down:* Please!

EMILY, *hands her the phone:* Here! Can you say who the father is?

SARAH: Well, ah . . . actually, yes. My husband . . .

EMILY: You have a *husband?*

SARAH: Last Tuesday.

EMILY: How fantastic! Make your call!

> *Watches with unwilling envy as Sarah goes to a space and calls.*

PHIL: Listen, I'm trustworthy, can you tell me the secret?—what am I shooting?

EMILY, *indicates the cross:* That.

PHIL: What am I supposed to do with that?

EMILY: Well, nothing, until they nail a man to it.

> *Soldiers lower the cross to the ground and start attaching a footrest . . . as . . .*

PHIL: I always knew you were gutsy, but doesn't this crowd insanity? You're not serious, are you?

EMILY: I may not be your director in about ten minutes, Phil. *To Skip:* . . . Which reminds me, do you have a doctor?

SKIP: Oh god, you're not feeling well?

EMILY: Not for me, for him! —You've really gone crazy, haven't you . . .

SKIP: I am not at all crazy! . . . In all the thousands of paintings and the written accounts of the crucifixion scene I defy anyone to produce a single one that shows a doctor present! I'm sorry but we can't be twisting the historical record! *Great new idea.* . . . And furthermore, I will not superimpose American mores on a dignified foreign people. The custom here is to crucify criminals, period! I am not about to condescend to these people with a foreign colonialist mentality!

EMILY: What about a hat?

SKIP: A hat?

EMILY: If I know mountains it'll probably be a hundred de-grees up here by noon.

SKIP: Yes, but a hat—is that the look we want?—on a cross with a hat? I mean we're not here to make some kind of a *comment*. I defy anyone to find a painting where he's wearing a . . .

EMILY: And what do you plan on giving him?

SKIP: Giving him . . . ?

EMILY: For the pain!

SKIP: If you're talking light drugs, okay, but we can't have him staggering up to the cross or something. Especially in like dry states . . . Kansas or whatever.

SARAH, *holding the phone:* They gave him wine, you know—the Romans . . .

SKIP: Well a little wine, but he can't look stoned. I mean we've got several million born-agains watching. Actually, I was thinking aspirin . . . or Tylenol if he's allergic . . .

EMILY: Aspirin with nails through his hands and feet? Skip dear, are you out of your fucking head? —I mean I personally am on the verge of disappearing here, but. . . . Look, I don't know why I'm even talking to you!

SKIP, *terror raised a notch:* Emily, dear, in all solemnity—if you walk on this one you'd better forget about any more work from us! And probably most if not all the other agencies. Now that's candid. It's simply too late to get somebody else, and your career, I can assure you is a wipeout.

EMILY: You are threatening me, Skip.

SKIP: I'm in no way threatening, dear, but if I know Thomson, Weber, Macdean and Abramowitz a lawsuit is not out of the question, and you'll be total roadkill in the industry!

Enter Felix in uniform, with the Captain.

FELIX: Henri! Good!—you've decided to come, what a nice surprise. Good morning all! —Have you met Mr. Cheeseboro? Mister Cheeseboro, Mr. Schultz, my cousin.

SKIP: We've met.

HENRI, *taking Felix's elbow—intimately:* Felix, I beg you . . . we must talk before you commit to this.

FELIX: Later. I have a problem.

HENRI: What do you mean?

FELIX: Everything is under control . . .

HENRI: What are you talking about?

But Felix has spotted Emily and is instantly vibrating.

FELIX, *both open hands toward her:* And who is . . . ?

SKIP: . . . Our director, sir—Emily Shapiro.

EMILY: How do you do.

FELIX, *sweeps his hat off his head, lowering it for an instant, hiding his "enthusiasm":* Wonderful! I hadn't expected a *woman* . . .

SARAH, *at one side with her phone:* Why not! I assure you women can film crucifixions as well as anybody else!

FELIX: I'm sure, but . . . *to Emily, while putting his hat back on.* . . . watching them, you know, can make even strong men uncomfortable.

EMILY: Oh? . . . Is this something you do fairly often?

FELIX, *points skyward:* That depends on the weather . . .

SKIP, *warm academic objectivity:* Now isn't that *interesting.*

FELIX: Most of our people are peasants, you see. *A shake of the fist.* When the crops are good, people are content. *Points skyward.* But it's hardly rained for twenty-six months, so there is a certain amount of unrest; we have an old saying, "when the rain stops the crosses sprout." It is not something we enjoy, I assure you, but there is either order or chaos. Are you taken for dinner?

EMILY: I hadn't thought about it. . . . I hope you won't mind too much, but I've half decided to try to stop this travesty from happening.

SKIP: That is not for you to . . . !

EMILY, *over-shouting him:* . . . Just so my crew and I—and especially Mr. Cheeseboro—know what to expect—when they're being nailed up do they like . . . *scream*?

HENRI: Certainly.

EMILY: And for how long?

FELIX: Not very; usually they're given a couple of bottles of tequila beforehand. Incidentally, I particularly admire your haircut.

SKIP: But you don't mean they're like . . . staggering.

HENRI: Of course.

FELIX: That is nonsense, Henri. Occasionally they have to be carried to the cross, but . . .

SKIP: Well that's out of the question . . .

FELIX: Oh? Why?

SKIP: Carrying him up to the cross would be like . . . I don't know . . . blasphemous in the United States!

EMILY: Sounds terrific to me . . . piggyback!

SKIP: Now wait, dear . . . !

EMILY: . . . Stop calling me "dear," my name is mud. Miss Mud. Emily Mud. *To Felix:* I'm sorry, General Whatever, but I've lost my brain.

FELIX: Haha—it's certainly not noticeable!

SKIP: Moving on to screaming, Mr. President—just to reassure our director—I assume it's important to this man what kind of public impression he makes, right?

FELIX: I have no idea; he has refused to say a word since he was caught.

SKIP: —But I should think if he is confident that he is about to . . . like meet his father in heaven, you could put it to him as a test of his faith that he not scream on camera. The camera, you see, tends to magnify everything and screaming on camera could easily seem in questionable taste.

FELIX: I understand. I will certainly try to discuss it with him.

SKIP: He cannot scream on camera, sir; it would destroy the whole effect. And I'm afraid I'll have to go further—I mean, sir, you have deposited our check, right? I mean as a man of honor . . .

FELIX: I will certainly do all I can to convince him not to scream.

HENRI, *turning Felix by the elbow—sotto:* What problem were you talking about?

EMILY: Well let's not nail him, so screaming is not a problem, right? *To both:* I said is that right?

SKIP, *to Emily:* All I'm trying to say, dear . . .

EMILY: Mud. When Emily is sued her name is Mud, so make it Mud, please!

SKIP, *momentarily put down:* I am simply saying that even though he was nailed—the Original, I mean—he is always shown hanging up there in perfect peace.

FELIX: The paintings are not like it is.

SARAH, *still with the phone:* What about the little sign over his head?

SKIP: What sign?

EMILY: Say that's right, they mocked him and stuck this hand-painted sign on the cross over his head—I believe it said "King of the Jews."

SKIP: No!! Absolutely out of the question . . . this has nothing to do with the Jews! Or Jesus either!

HENRI: Excuse me, but it will inevitably have that connotation.

SKIP: Nonsense! This is simply the execution of a violent criminal!

HENRI: Yes, but isn't that what they said the first time?

SARAH, *phone to her ear:* Speaking of Jews, they called him "rabbi," I think.

SKIP: Stop it! —Excuse me, Emily, no reflection on your personal heritage, but I mean, this will run in like Mississippi and even the Middle East, like Egypt . . . we do a lot of business in Egypt and Pakistan, and there's no point irritating the world's largest religion—I mean, from their viewpoint it's bad enough implying the son of god was Christian without making him Jewish, for Heaven's sake.

EMILY: All right, but I'm just saying—he . . . *was* . . .

SKIP: You know it and I know it, dear, but what's the point of rubbing it in worldwide, darling? *Turning to Felix:* Now sir, have you decided what time of the day you are going to . . . ah . . . there's a question of the light, you see.

FELIX: I'm not sure we will be able to proceed today. It is possible, but perhaps not.

SKIP: I don't understand, sir.

FELIX: He's escaped.

EMILY: Our guy?

HENRI, *a clap of his hands:* Felix!

FELIX: He will certainly be captured, there's no question, but it may be a day or two . . .

EMILY, *to the crew:* He's escaped!

CREW: Attaway, baby! Hurray! etc. . . . .

SKIP: Shame on you! The man's a criminal! *To Felix:* This is terrible, terrible news, General! CNN, NBC . . .

Soldier starts up a screaming chainsaw.

FELIX: Para! Esta puta cosa. Para! [English: Stop that goddam thing! I said stop it!]

Soldier, dumbfounded, cuts saw.

CAPTAIN: No ves que están hablando? [English: Can't you see they're talking?]

Soldier salutes in terror.

Eres un imbécil? [English: Are you an idiot?]

Soldier salutes again.

HENRI, *touching Felix's arm:* Listen, Felix . . .

FELIX, *freeing his arm:* I want to offer to pay for the extra time you will be here, Mr. Skip, but he will absolutely be found by tomorrow, maybe tonight.

SKIP: I am only concerned about our exclusivity, any delay is dangerous. *To the crew:* I want everyone at the hotel . . . we meet let's say noon, or make it eleven, and we'll see where we are. And don't wander off in case he's caught sooner.

FELIX: . . . I believe we will catch him even this afternoon, maybe.

As crew packs, preparing—with uncertainty—to leave, he turns back to Skip.

Not to worry about the exclusivity, I have the Army blocking the only road up this mountain; no other crew can get up here.

SKIP: There are helicopters.

FELIX: I have forbidden any takeoffs.

SKIP: What about from over the border?

FELIX: They cross the border they will be shot happily down.

SKIP: Well that's a relief. *To Emily:* How about lunch and let's talk?

EMILY: I think I'll have a look around the country for a bit . . .

SKIP: Don't go far . . . please. *To Felix:* I'm expecting your call the moment you have any news, sir.

FELIX: Rest assured. *Skip exits. To Emily:* Then may I expect you for dinner, Miss Shapiro? I was serious about your haircut, I find it very moving in a way that is particularly important to me.

EMILY: A moving haircut!—in that case, yes, I'd love dinner . . .

FELIX: Until tonight then, Miss Shapiro!

> *He gets to the periphery where Henri intercepts him—intimately.*

HENRI: What happened?

FELIX: I can't talk about it.

HENRI: Well, how did he get out?

FELIX: He paid off the guards.

HENRI: Where'd he get the money?

FELIX: How the hell would I know! —They're trying to hand me this bullshit that he walked through the walls. They're calling him a magician, but he paid them off and I've locked them all up and I'm going to find that little bastard if I do nothing else in my life!

He starts out; Henri grabs his arm.

HENRI: Felix! Do nothing! Thank your lucky stars, it's a blessing.

FELIX, *loudly, angered:* A blessing? It's chaos! —And I'm going to miss my analysis day in Miami!

Felix throws off Henri's hand, goes to Emily, kisses her hand.

Again! —Until tonight, Miss Shapiro!

With a gallant wave he exits. Henri starts to follow, but halts and turns to Emily.

HENRI: You could stop this, you know.

EMILY: Me!

HENRI: Couldn't you try to dissuade him? Seriously—he can be very affected by good-looking women. He's undergoing psychoanalysis now. I've never known him to be quite this ambivalent about things—last year he'd have shot this man by now. And to be candid, I thought his reaction to meeting you was amazingly genuine . . . I mean his feeling.

EMILY: And he did like my haircut.

HENRI: He's a big baby, you know; his mother nursed him till he was seven.

EMILY: I hope you don't expect me to pick up where she left off.

SARAH, *closing her phone:* I'm pregnant!

EMILY: Oh, Sarah!

She bursts into tears.

SARAH: What's the matter? *Taking her hand as she weeps loudly, uncontrolled.* Oh Emily, what is it!

EMILY: I'm so glad for you! I mean you look so happy and I'm all fucked up! Kisses Sarah. Drink milk or something . . .

HENRI: I do admire your irony!

EMILY: Yes, I'm famous for it. Miss Irony Mud. —Okay, I'll margarine the General.

HENRI: Thank you, my dear.

EMILY: Tell me, Henri, as a truth-loving philosopher—wouldn't you gladly resign from the human race if only there was another one to belong to?

HENRI: Oh, of course. But are we sure it would be any better?

Blackout.

SCENE 3

*Stanley, an apostle, softly plays a harmonica in Felix's
office. Sneakers, unkempt ponytail, blue denim shirt,
backpack.*

Felix enters.

FELIX: Thank you for coming.

STANLEY: Well, I was arrested.

FELIX: What's your name again?

STANLEY: Stanley.

FELIX: You know who I am.

STANLEY: Of course. You're the head.

FELIX: Tha-a-a-t's right, I am the head. I'm told you're very
close to him.

STANLEY, *cautiously:* You could say that.

FELIX: Asshole buddies.

STANLEY: . . . I never put it quite that way.

FELIX: I'm told you did some . . . service for us a while back.

STANLEY: I've made some mistakes in my life, that was one of the big ones.

FELIX: We need to know where he is. There's good money in the information.

STANLEY: Thanks, but I really don't need money right now.

FELIX: Then tell me gratis—where is he?

STANLEY: I've no idea. Honest.

FELIX: A neighbor claims he saw him going into your house in the middle of last night.

STANLEY: How did he know it was him?

FELIX: He'd seen him earlier, standing on the corner staring into space for over an hour like a crazy man.

STANLEY: He only stayed with me a little and left.

FELIX: . . . Tell me, does *he* think he's the son of god?

STANLEY: That depends.

FELIX: Really! On what?

STANLEY: Hard to say.

FELIX: Let's put it this way, Stanley, if you're going to fuck around with me we'll be happy to knock your teeth out, starting with the front. This would not be my preference, but we are a military government and I am only one of five officers running things. Now please answer my questions before some really bad personalities get into this. The question is whether he believes he is the son of god.

STANLEY: Some days he's sure of it and then he . . . suddenly can't believe it. I mean it's understandable.

FELIX: Why is it understandable?

STANLEY: Well, a man facing crucifixion'd better be pretty sure what he believes.

FELIX: Why? If he's the son of god crucifixion shouldn't bother him too much.

STANLEY: Yeah, but if it turns out he's not the son of god it'll bother him a lot.

FELIX: What's your opinion? Is he?

STANLEY: . . . I better fill you in before I answer that. I've ruined my life believing in things; I spent two and a half years in India in an ashram; I've been into everything from dope to alcohol to alfalfa therapy to Rolfing to Buddhism to total vegetarianism, which I'm into now. So you ask me do I believe he's the son of god, I have to be honest—yes, I believe he is . . . kind of.

FELIX: Kind of.

STANLEY: Well, with a background like mine how do I know what I'm going to believe next week?

FELIX, *thinks for a moment:* What did you talk about with him last night?

STANLEY: Last night? Well, let's see—women, mainly. They're a mystery to him. Men also, but not as much.

FELIX: He's bisexual?

STANLEY: I would say he's more like . . . tri.

FELIX: Trisexual.

STANLEY: Yes.

FELIX: Well let's see now—there's men, and women, and what?

STANLEY: Well . . . vegetation.

FELIX: He fucks cabbages?

STANLEY: No-no, he loves them.

FELIX: Loves cabbages.

STANLEY: Well they're alive.

FELIX: I see. What about a girlfriend?

STANLEY: Well, yeah, one. But she jumped out of a window recently.

FELIX: . . . You don't mean Henri Schultz's daughter.

STANLEY: Oh, you know him?

FELIX: We're cousins. —So this son of god is banging Schultz's daughter?

STANLEY: I don't think so, frankly. My impression is that it stays kind of—you know—remote. Although I picked him up one morning at her apartment and she looked like a woman who . . . you know . . .

FELIX: Had had it.

STANLEY: But I think it was different. I think he may have just . . . laid down next to her and . . . you know . . . lit up. —Because you know he can just light up and . . .

FELIX: I know, I saw him do it. So you mean if he lights up it makes her . . . ?

STANLEY: Definitely.

FELIX, *truly fascinated:* Huh! That's very interesting. That's one of the most interesting things I've heard lately. —And how long can he stay lit up?

STANLEY: Seems like . . . I don't know . . . a few seconds.

FELIX: Is that all.

STANLEY: Well of course I never actually saw . . .

FELIX: So it could have been longer.

STANLEY: Who knows? I mean . . .

FELIX: Yes. *Exhales, blows out air.* This is really amazing. *Worried but curious.* I was wondering why Schultz was so fascinated by him.

STANLEY: Oh but I doubt she'd have mentioned Jack to her father.

FELIX: That's his name—Jack?

STANLEY: Well one of them. Jack Brown. But he's got others . . . depending.

FELIX: We believe his name is Juan Manuel Francisco Frederico Ortuga de Oviedo. Although up in the villages some of them call him Ralph.

STANLEY: Possible. He changes names so he won't turn into like . . . you know . . . some kind of celebrity guru.

FELIX: Well, that's unusual, isn't it. Now tell me how he escaped from jail.

STANLEY: I really can't talk about that.

FELIX: How did he get out, Stanley?

STANLEY: He doesn't like people talking about it.

FELIX: About what?

STANLEY, *conflicted, shifts in his chair:* I'm really not comfortable talking about that part of it.

FELIX: I don't want to have to persuade you, Stan. How did he escape?

STANLEY: Well . . . is this something you're insisting on?

FELIX: This is something I'm insisting on.

STANLEY: . . . He went through the walls.

Pause.

FELIX: And how did he do that?

STANLEY: You're asking me so I'm telling you, right? He has terrific mind control, he can see space.

FELIX: Anybody can see space.

STANLEY: No. What you see is the borders, like the walls of a room, or mountains. Pure space is only an idea, so he can think it out of existence. But he doesn't want it spread around too much.

FELIX: Why's that?

STANLEY: If he gets known as a magician he thinks it could take away from his main message.

FELIX: Which is what, in a few words?

STANLEY: Well, you know . . . just don't do bad things. Especially when you know they're bad. Which you mostly do.

Pause.

FELIX: You like women?

STANLEY: Well I'm . . . yeah, I guess I'm kind of on the horny side.

FELIX: You ever light up with them?

STANLEY: Me? Well there've been times when I almost feel I have, but . . . I guess I've never *blinded* any of them.

FELIX, *some embarrassment:* I want to talk to him, Stanley. For personal reasons.

STANLEY: Well, if he shows up, I'll tell him.

FELIX, *attempting cool:* . . . I want you to emphasize the personal. Let him pick a place and I'll meet him alone.

STANLEY, *realizing:* . . . Oh!

FELIX: I'm interested in discussing the *whole* situation. You understand?

STANLEY: —Okay, I'll tell him. —You want to be any more specific?

FELIX, *hesitates:* . . . No, that's . . . that's about it. *Suddenly suspicious, hardens.* He didn't send you to me, did he?

Stanley looks away.

Stanley?

No response.

Did he send you?

No response.

Why did he send you?

No response.

Answer me! Did you get yourself arrested?

STANLEY: It's complicated. —I can't stand the idea of him being . . . you know . . . hurt. So I thought maybe I could talk to you about it. —See, I think in some part of his mind he thinks it would help the people.

FELIX: If he's executed.

STANLEY: Crucified.

FELIX: He wants it.

STANLEY: . . . In a way, maybe.

FELIX: How would it help them?

STANLEY: Well, now that the revolution's practically gone, people are pretty . . . you know . . . cynical about everything.

FELIX: What about it?

STANLEY: To see a man tortured for their sake . . . you know . . . that a man could actually like care that much about anything . . .

FELIX: You're telling me something . . . what are you telling me? —Does he want it or not?

STANLEY: Oh no! No. It's just that . . . you see— *Rapidly overwhelmed by the vision's horror.* —he gets to where he just can't like bear it—

FELIX: Bear what!

STANLEY: Well . . . the horror!

FELIX: What horror, what the hell are you talking about!

STANLEY: Well like—excuse the expression—living in this country! Like when he takes a walk and sees some—some guy sending out eight-year-old daughters to work the streets, or those little kids a couple of weeks ago killing that old man for his shoes . . . Or, excuse the expression, the Army opening up on that farmers' demonstration last spring . . .

FELIX: Those people had no permission to . . . !

STANLEY, *more and more stridently:* Well you asked me so I'm telling you, right? A massacre like that can start him shivering and he can't stop crying! I've seen him go for . . . like two hours at a time, crying his heart out. Then he stops and he's cool for a while. We even have fun. Then he sees something and it like hits him again and he begins talking like in . . . Swedish, sounds like, or Russian or German—he once told me in a joke that he's trying to find out what language god understands. Then he falls asleep, and wakes up sounding like anybody else—and that's when he doesn't know.

FELIX: Doesn't know what?

STANLEY: Well . . . whether maybe he really is supposed to die, and . . . like cause everything to change. —I mean, for your own sake, sir, I would definitely think about just letting him go, you know? I mean this can be dangerous!

FELIX: I think you know where he is, Stanley. I asked you in a nice way, now we'll try something else.

Goes to the door, grasps the knob.

STANLEY: You going to hurt me?

FELIX: I'm stashing you away until you make up your mind to lead us to him. And incidentally, there's some hungry livestock in there that I don't think you're going to enjoy. Get in!

Felix opens the door and the blinding white light flies out; he raises his hands to shield his eyes.

My god, he's back!

Stanley falls to his knees facing the open door. Felix steps to his desk, presses a button, loud alarm bells go off as he shouts into his intercom . . .

Captain! Come quick, he's back, he's back!

Captain and two soldiers come in on the run.

Captain and soldiers rush out through the door. Felix yanks Stanley to his feet.

FELIX: Why did he come back? What's this all about, Stanley?

STANLEY, *scared, elevated:* God knows!

FELIX, *grabs Stanley, shakes him:* Answer me! Answer me!

STANLEY, *almost lifted off the floor by the throat:* —I think he just can't make up his mind, that's all—whether he really wants to—like die. I mean it's understandable, right?—

Felix releases him.

. . . with this great kind of weather we're having?

Captain and two soldiers back out of the cell door-way; they are trembling, trailing their rifles, staring in at the cell.

FELIX: What's this now!

He rushes to the cell, looks in. Then turns to the soldiers.

How'd he get out!

They are speechless. Whirls about to Stanley.

Talk to me! Why'd he come back! Why'd he escape?

STANLEY: I don't know! . . . Maybe to get your mind off me?
I mean . . . it's possible, right?—for a friend?

Blackout.

SCENE 4

Café table. Henri seated with a bottle of water and glass. Skip enters, looking about.

HENRI: Mr. Cheeseboro!

SKIP: Hi. *Sitting.* I don't have much time. What can you tell me?

HENRI: Can I order something?

SKIP: I'll have to leave in a few minutes.

HENRI: No news, I take it.

SKIP: Nothing. And you?

HENRI, *a shake of the head:* I thought an exchange of ideas could be useful—the two of us, quietly . . .

SKIP, *slaps his own cheeks then lets his head hang:* I'm beginning to smell the dead-dog stink of disaster. *Straightens up.* Tell me—why'd the General let this man escape?

HENRI: It was a complete surprise to him. I spoke to him shortly after it happened; he was absolutely shocked . . .

SKIP: But he had him locked in a cell. —We've made a large down-payment, you know. . . . Or may one appeal to logic in this country?

HENRI: This is why I thought you and I ought to talk.

SKIP: About what?

HENRI: Have you any interest in history? Or philosophy? Where did you go to school?

SKIP: Princeton. But my interest was business, frankly. No philosophy, no culture, mainly the market.

HENRI: Oh, but poetry and the stock market have a lot in common, you know.

SKIP: *Poetry and the market!*

HENRI: Oh yes. They are both based on rules that the successful never obey. —A few years ago I spent some time in Egypt . . . you've probably been there?

SKIP: Egypt?—I've shot commercials all over Egypt . . . Chrysler, Bayer Aspirin, Viagra . . .

HENRI: . . . Then you know some of the wall paintings and sculpture.

SKIP: Of course. —What's this about?

HENRI: I want to tell you about a surprising discovery I made there. I am far from expert on the subject, but . . .

SKIP: What are you, a businessman or an academic?

HENRI: I retired from the pharmaceuticals business some years ago. I still breed fighting bulls but I'm getting out of that too; I'm basically a scholar now. In Egypt . . .

SKIP, *takes out a cell phone and punches numbers from notebook:* Excuse me.

HENRI: If you're making a local call . . .

SKIP: The General's office. To tell him I'm here.

HENRI: Doubt that'll work . . . *Glances at watch.* . . . this close to lunch.

SKIP: Good god, why don't they fix it?

HENRI: They? There is no "they" here; hasn't been in most of the world since the fall of Rome.

SKIP, *snaps his phone shut:* What can you tell me about this guy's escape?

HENRI: —I know how absurd this is going to sound, but I ask you to hear me out. *Slight pause.* I had a very distinct feeling at the time they found him gone, that he had never been in that cell.

SKIP: But they had him, they'd captured him.

HENRI: They believed that, yes.

SKIP: What are you talking about?

HENRI, *considers:*. . . It struck me one day in Egypt . . .

SKIP, *starting to rise:* Look, I have no interest in Egypt . . .

HENRI, *voice hardly raised*: This may save your neck, Mr. Cheeseboro! Do sit; please.—

Skip goes still.

It struck me one day; that there were lots of images of the peoples the Egyptians had conquered, but none showing Jewish captives. I am far from expert in the subject but I couldn't find more than one or two menorah—candelabra—a vague star of David . . . almost nothing, really. Which is terribly strange when the Jews are supposed to have drowned the whole Egyptian army, don't you think? And Joseph was the Pharaoh's chief adviser and so on? It would be, let's say, like writing the history of Japan with no mention of the atomic bomb.—

SKIP: But what is the connection with . . . ?

HENRI: One day the thought hit me—could the whole story of the Jews in Egypt have simply been a poem? More or less like Homer describing magical cattle, and ravenous women and so on? Ancient peoples saw no difference between a vivid description of marvels and what we call reality—for them the description itself *was* the reality. In short, the Jews may never have been literally enslaved in Egypt; or perhaps *some* had been, but the story as we know it may have been largely fictional, an overwhelmingly powerful act of the imagination.

SKIP: If you're telling me this guy doesn't exist, I'm . . .

HENRI: That depends on what you mean by "exist"; he certainly exists in the mind of the desperately poor peasant—he is the liberator; for the General his crucifixion will powerfully reinforce good order, so he must exist . . . and I know a suicidal young woman of high intelligence who insists that he has restored her will to live, so for her he certainly exists. And needless to say, for you, of course . . . his execution will sell some very expensive advertising, so you are committed to his existing.

SKIP: But he can't be imaginary, the General spoke with him.

HENRI: Not quite. According to the General the fellow never said a single word. Not one. The General spoke *at* him.

SKIP: But didn't I hear of this . . . apostle of his they've just jailed? *He's* certainly spoken with him.

HENRI: A fellow named Stanley, yes. I understand he is a drug addict. I needn't say more; he could be put away for the rest of his life unless he cooperates. Drug-taking is a felony in this country.

SKIP: Really. But they export tons of it.

HENRI: They do indeed. The logic is as implacable as it is beyond anyone's comprehension.

SKIP: Then what are you telling me? —Because you've gotta believe it, the money we paid the General is not a poem.

HENRI: But it may turn into one as so many other important things have done. The Vietnam War, for example, began . . .

SKIP: The Vietnam War!

HENRI: . . . Which was set off, mind you, by a night attack upon a United States warship by a Vietnamese gunboat in the Gulf of Tonkin. It's now quite certain the attack never happened. This was a fiction, a poem; but fifty-six thousand Americans and two million Vietnamese had to die before the two sides got fed up reciting it.

SKIP: But what is this light . . . not that I'm sure I believe it . . . but he emits a light, I'm told.

HENRI: Yes. I saw it.

SKIP: You saw it!

HENRI: At the time I thought I did, yes. But I was primed beforehand by my two days in the upper villages where everyone is absolutely convinced he is god—so as I approached that cell door my brain *demanded* an astonishment and I believe I proceeded to create one.

SKIP: Meaning what?

HENRI: Mr. Cheeseboro, I have spent a lifetime trying to free myself from the boredom of reality. —Needless to say, I have badly hurt some people dear to me—as those who flee reality usually do. So what I am about to tell you has cost me. —I am convinced now apart from getting fed, most human activity—sports, opera, TV, movies, dressing up, dressing down—or just going for a walk—has no other purpose than to deliver us into the realm of the imagination. The imagination is a great hall where death, for example, turns into a painting, and a scream of pain becomes a song. The hall of the imagination is really where we usually live; and this is all right except for one thing—to enter that hall one must leave one's real sorrow at the door and in its stead surround oneself with images and words and music that mimic anguish but are really drained of it—no one has ever lost a leg from reading about a battle, or died of hearing the saddest song. *Close to tears.* And this is why . . .

SKIP: I don't see why . . .

HENRI, *overriding:* . . . This is why this man must be hunted down and crucified; because—*he still really feels everything.* Imagine, Mr. Cheeseboro, if that kind of reverence for life should spread! Governments would collapse, armies disband, marriages disintegrate! Wherever we turned, our dead un-feeling shallowness would stare us in the face until we shriv-eled up with shame! No!—better to hunt him down and kill him and leave us in peace.

SKIP: . . . You're addressing me, aren't you.

HENRI: Oh, and myself, I assure you a thousand, thousand times myself.

SKIP: On the other hand, shallow as I am I have twins registered at Andover; maybe some need to be shallow so that some can be deep.

He starts to rise.

HENRI: Please! Go home!

SKIP: I can't go home until this job is done!

HENRI: You could tell your company there was nothing here to photograph! It was all imaginary, a poem!

SKIP: It's impossible, I can't pull out of this.

Starts off.

HENRI: I hope you won't take offense!

Skip halts, turns, curious.

Our generals are outraged, a cageful of tigers roaring for meat! *Somebody* may get himself crucified—and not necessarily a man who has done anything. Do you want the responsibility for helping create that injustice!

SKIP: I've been trying hard not to resent you, Mr. Schultz, but this I resent. —I am not "creating" anything! I am no more responsible for this situation than Matthew, Mark, Luke and John were for Jesus' torture!

HENRI: But Jesus was already long dead when they wrote about him, he was beyond harm!

SKIP: Well, I can't see the difference.

HENRI: But Mr. Cheeseboro, this man is still alive!

SKIP: We are recording a preexisting fact, Mr. Schultz, not creating it—I create nothing!

HENRI: But the fortune you've paid the General has locked him into this monstrous thing! Your money is critical in his decision!

SKIP, *exploding:* You have utterly wasted my time!

He exits.

HENRI: And so the poem continues, written in someone's blood, and my country sinks one more inch into the grass, into the jungle, into the everlasting sea.

Blackout.

SCENE 5

Darkness. A moon. A palm tree. Light rises, gradually revealing a candelabra on a café table, with Felix and Emily eating lobsters and drinking wine.

At all the dim edges of the stage, riflemen sit crouched, weapons at the ready, backs to the couple.

Music; very distant strains of a guitar and singers serenading.

EMILY: I've never in my life eaten three lobsters.

FELIX: But they're very small, no?

EMILY: Even so.

FELIX: Of course, small things can be better than big sometimes.

EMILY: Oh? *Catches on.* Oh, of course, yes!

FELIX: I beg you to forgive my forwardness.

EMILY: Not at all—I like it.

FELIX: I can't help myself, I am desperate for you not to slip away.

They eat in silence, sucking the lobster legs.

EMILY: You're a contradictory person, aren't you?

FELIX: I have never thought so; why am I contradictory?

EMILY: Well, you seem so tough, but you're also very sentimental.

FELIX: Perhaps, yes. But with very few people. This is a hard country to govern.

EMILY: —I must say, your face seems softer than when we met.

FELIX: Possibly because something grips my imagination as we converse.

EMILY: Grips your imagination?

FELIX: Your body. —I beg you to forgive my frankness, it's because I am sure, Emily, that I could . . . how shall I say . . . function with you.

EMILY, *equivocally:* Well now . . .

FELIX: How fantastic—you are blushing! *She laughs nervously.* My god, how your spirit speaks to me! There is something sacred in you, Emily—for for me it's as though you descended from the air. —I must sound like I have lost my mind, but could you stay on some weeks? Or months? I have everything here for you . . .

EMILY: I'm afraid I have too many obligations at home. And I'm going to have to get busy saving my career. *Pointedly.* . . . Unless you'd decide to do what I asked.

FELIX: I beg you, my dear, you can't ask me to call off the search. The General Staff would never stand for it . . .

EMILY: But if you insisted . . .

FELIX: It's impossible; the honor of the Armed Forces is at stake. This man is trying to make fools of us.

EMILY, *reaches out and touches his cheek. Surprised, he instantly grasps her hand and kisses her palm.* Why do I think you don't want to catch him, Felix . . . you personally?

FELIX, *cradles his face in her palm:* . . . To tell you the truth I'm not sure anymore what I want.

EMILY: . . . Just out of curiosity, you really think my haircut started it?

FELIX: Oh yes, absolutely, it went straight to my heart.

EMILY: Imagine. And here I was thinking it was too short.

FELIX: No—no, it's perfect! I had one look and it was as though I . . . I was rising from the dead.

EMILY: . . . Could we talk about that?

FELIX: About what, my dear?

EMILY: The . . . ah . . . difficulty you have that you've been . . . alluding to.

FELIX, *fear and eager curiosity:* What about it?

EMILY: . . . Unless you don't feel . . .

FELIX, *steeling himself; deeply curious:* . . . No—no, of course not, I have no fear!

EMILY: Well, what I think, is that you have to seem invulnerable to the world, and so you suppress your feelings.

FELIX: I am running a country, Emily, I cannot expose my feelings to . . .

EMILY: I know, but that suppression has spread down and down and down . . . *Running her finger up his arm and down his chest:* until it's finally clobbered . . . your willy. *Quickly.* You're simply going to have to let your feelings out, Felix, is all I'm saying.

FELIX, *aroused and confused:* I am . . . I am . . . I . . . I . . . *Disarming himself.* . . . must talk to you . . . I can come to New York, I have money there and an apartment . . .

EMILY: Why wait? Like if you feel you really don't wish to pursue this fellow, just don't do it and see what happens.

FELIX: Darling, the General Staff would tear me apart, they are hungry lions . . .

EMILY, *reaches for his hand:* Felix dear . . . I don't know where this is going between us, but I must tell you now—if you go through with this outrage you'll have to find yourself another girl. —Not that I'm promising anything in any case.

FELIX: But what are your feelings toward me? You never speak of them.

EMILY: I like a man to be a man, Felix—which you are. And I have enormous curiosity.

FELIX: About men.

EMILY: Yes. Powerful men, especially . . . to tell the truth.

FELIX: About what in particular?

EMILY: Well, frankly, for one thing—how they are making love.

FELIX: I have never known a woman with such courage to speak her mind.

EMILY: One needs it when one is not marvelous to look at.

FELIX, *kisses her hand:* You are more marvelous to look at than . . . than six mountains and a waterfall!

EMILY: That's very sweet of you, Felix. —I'd love to walk along the beach. Could we, without all these guards?

FELIX: I'm afraid not. But come, we can take a few steps through the garden.

They walk together.

EMILY: Who exactly would want to kill you, Communists?

FELIX: The Party is split on this question. One side thinks somebody worse would replace me if I am eliminated.

EMILY: And I suppose the Right Wing people love you . . .

FELIX: Not all—some of them think I am not hard enough on the Communists . . . those might take a shot at me too. Then there are the narco-guerillas; with some we have an arrangement, it's no secret, but there are others who are not happy for various reasons.

EMILY: It all seems so utterly, utterly futile. Or do you mind?

He halts, holds her hand.

FELIX: I mind very much, in these hours since I know you. Very much. You have made me wish that I could live differently.

EMILY: Really!

FELIX: Emily, I will confess to you—when I imagine myself making love to you, entering into you, I . . . I almost hear a choir.

EMILY: A choir! Really, Felix, that is beautiful!

Felix suddenly turns away, covering his eyes.

EMILY: What is it? You all right? Felix?

Felix straightens up, grasps her hand, kisses it, holds it to his cheek.

EMILY: What is it?

FELIX: I will divorce.

EMILY, *blurting:* Oh no, you mustn't do that! . . . I mean you're a Catholic, aren't you?

FELIX: I am ready to go to hell! I cannot lose you!

EMILY: But my dear, I'm not prepared for . . . I assume you're talking commitment?

FELIX, *striking his chest:* You have exploded in my mind like a grenade! I have never had such a feeling . . . it is like all my windows have blown out and a fresh breeze is passing through me . . . I must not let you go, Emily—what can I give you! Anything! Tell me!

EMILY: Ralph!

FELIX: Ralph?

EMILY: Let him go!

FELIX, *at the height of tension—dives:* That is what you truly wish?

EMILY: Oh yes, Felix—yes! It would solve everything for me! And he sounds like such a dear person!

FELIX: And you will surely see me in New York.

EMILY: Of course, I'll be happy to!—I mean not necessarily on a permanent basis . . . I mean I travel a lot, but . . . yes, of course!

FELIX: All right, then—it is done!

EMILY: Done! Oh, Felix, I'm overwhelmed!

FELIX: I have fallen in love with you, Emily! Come—let me take you to my best house.

EMILY: Your best?

FELIX, *solemnly:* It was my mother's. I have never brought anyone there before. It is sacred to me. I haven't been there since I was seven.

EMILY: That's very touching. But first could we go into the mountains? I would like to see one of those high villages where they love this Ralph fellow so. It's just an experience I've never had, have you?—to walk in a place full of love? *Up close to him, face raised.* Take me there, Felix?

FELIX, *sensing her distant surrender:* My god, woman—yes, anything! Come . . . come to the mountains!

He grips her hand and they hurry off with all the guards following, their heads revolving in all directions in the search for killers.

Blackout.

SCENE 6

Jeanine rises from her wheelchair with help of a cane, and walks with a limp to a point. Henri enters, stands, astonished.

HENRI: Jeanine!

She turns to him.

JEANINE: I don't understand it. I woke up, and I was standing.

HENRI: And the pain?

JEANINE: It seems much less. For the moment anyway.

HENRI: This is absolutely astonishing, Jeanine. This is marvelous! How did this happen?

JEANINE: The lightning this morning shot a lot of electricity into the air—

HENRI: —Could that have affected you?

JEANINE, *cryptically:* I . . . don't know, really.

Pause. Henri settles in.

HENRI: I'm sorry, dear, but we have to talk about Felix.

JEANINE: Oh god, why?

HENRI: He called me this morning—woke me at dawn. He's convinced you can lead him to this god-fellow.

Jeanine is silent.

He'll be here to see you this morning. He insisted. *Coming to his point.* . . . Do you know a fellow named Stanley?

JEANINE, *hedging:* Stanley.

HENRI: They have him.

She stiffens.

He has apparently told Felix you and this . . . god-fellow are lovers.

She is silent.

Felix is convinced you would know where to find him.

JEANINE: Papa, I have no way of contacting this man, so let's just forget it, will you?

HENRI, *a moment; swallows resentment:* According to Felix this Stanley fellow has hinted that your friend may actually welcome crucifixion. In order to accomplish his . . . whatever it is . . . his mission.

Jeanine is silent.

In any case, I'm not sure I can keep you from being arrested for harboring him and failing to turn him in.

JEANINE: But how can I turn him in! I don't know how to contact him!

HENRI: . . . For one thing, darling—how shall I put it?—he clearly had to have been here last night . . .

JEANINE: Why!

HENRI, *patience gone:* Well look at you! Felix is not stupid, Jeanine—he knows your spine was crushed, it could only have been this man's hand on you that has brought you to life like this!

JEANINE: . . . You believe then!?

HENRI: . . . I don't know what I believe! I only know that Felix intends to kill this man and that can't be allowed to happen!

JEANINE: Oh Papa, why do you go on caring so much when you know you will never act! You'll never stand up to these murderers!

HENRI: Act how! Who do I join! How can you go on repeating that political nonsense? There is no politics anymore,

Jeanine—if you weren't so tough-minded you'd admit it! There is nothing, my dear, nothing but one's family, if one can call that a faith.

JEANINE: Late one night you came into my room and sat down on my bed. There was a storm. Tremendous! The wind broke limbs off the oak behind the house. It groaned, like pieces of the sky breaking off! And you said you had decided to go into the mountains and join the guerillas to fight against Felix! Lightning seemed to flash around your head, Papa. You were like a mountain, sitting there. At last you would do something, at last you would answer the idiots and fight against Felix! And I knew I would follow you . . . and high up in the mountains I found you in your tent with a rifle on your lap, reading Spinoza.

HENRI: The world will never again be changed by heroes; if I misled you I apologize to the depths of my heart. One must learn to live in the garden of one's self.

JEANINE: Even if one has seen god?

HENRI: . . . Then you really do believe?

JEANINE: I think so, yes.

HENRI: Very well. I'm glad.

JEANINE: You are!

HENRI: I'm happy for the love I see in you, my dear, your hair flowing so gently around your face, and the softness that I haven't seen in so many years in the corners of your eyes. I love you, Jeanine, and if it's he who brought you back to life . . . —Why not? I think now it is no more impossible than the rest of this dream we live in. *Glances at watch.* —Felix will be here soon. I'll wait with you, is that all right?

> *She suddenly weeps; he goes to his knees beside her.*

HENRI, *embracing her:* Oh my darling, my darling . . . !

> *Enter Felix, with Emily—her hand tucked under his arm. Henri springs up.*

Felix! Miss Shapiro! Good morning! Miss Shapiro, this is my daughter, Jeanine.

FELIX, *going to Jeanine in surprise:* Why Jeanine, how wonderfully well you look! My god, this is amazing—what's happened?

HENRI: Nothing. She often has more energy in the mornings.

FELIX: We must talk, Jeanine . . .

HENRI: She's really not up to it, Felix.

FELIX: There's a couple of things I'd like this man to understand. It's important.

HENRI: But she has no contact with him.

FELIX: Well, if you happen to see him—

HENRI, *glancing from one to the other:* —Something's happened, hasn't it . . . with you.

EMILY: Oh yes! We hardly slept all night.

HENRI: How nice!

EMILY: Yes . . . it was.

HENRI: Well! May one congratulate the old dog?

FELIX: Definitely!—he's back hunting over hill and dale. This is the strangest twenty-four hours I've ever been through.— *Drapes an arm around Emily.* . . . She wanted to drive up and look around in the villages . . .

EMILY: It's like walking on the sky up there—the purity of the sunbeams . . . that strangely warm, icy air . . .

FELIX: It's been years since I was up there in our last campaigns. I was absolutely amazed—his picture really is everywhere in the villages. They paint halos around his head. I had no idea of the devotion of the people—it's a real phenomenon, he's like a saint. *To Henri:* You remember, Henri—that whole back country was always so . . . what's the word . . . ?

HENRI: Depressing.

EMILY: They've taken out the ancient instruments that nobody has played for years, and they dance the old dances again. . . . It was so absolutely delightful, we didn't want to leave.

JEANINE: Then you've decided what?—not to kill him?

FELIX: I must have a meeting with him. I was hoping you could arrange it.

HENRI, *instantly:* She really has no idea where he . . .

FELIX, *charmingly to Jeanine:* One thing I'm never wrong about is the face of a satisfied woman. —When he comes to you again I would like him to understand the following: I have talked to a number of his people now and they say he has always told them to live in peace. Some of my own people say otherwise but I'm willing to leave it at that. What I want him to consider— I mean eventually, of course—is a place in the government.

JEANINE: In *your* government? *Him?*

FELIX: I'm serious. The military is not as stupid as maybe we've sometimes looked, Jeanine. We must get ready for some kind of democracy, now that the revolution is finished. He could help us in that direction.

JEANINE: I'd doubt that.

EMILY: He's released Stanley.

JEANINE: Really.

FELIX: Stanley's agreed to deliver my message to your friend, but I don't know how much weight he carries with him. I would feel better if you spoke to him yourself.

JEANINE: But I know his answer. He will tell you to resign.

FELIX: Resign.

JEANINE: —Let's be honest, Felix; this man is full of love—I think you realize that now, don't you; all he is is love. But we aren't. I'm not and neither are you. You've killed too many of us to forget so quickly.

FELIX: I have changed, Jeanine. This woman has opened my eyes.

JEANINE, *to Emily:* Imagine!—in one night!

FELIX: No, not one night; I've been thinking about it for some time now . . . that we've been fighting each other almost since I was born. It has wasted us all. I want a normal country. Where people can walk safely in the streets at night; sleep in peace, build a house . . . I can't tell you how exactly it happened, but this woman has made me wonder—maybe if your friend could help us begin to come together I am ready to give it a try. *He sees she is not convinced.*

What can I do to prove I have changed, Jeanine?

EMILY, *to Jeanine:* I have an idea . . . suppose he announced on television that your friend was no longer a wanted man?

FELIX: Excuse me, dear—I can't do that unless he agrees in advance to disarm *his* people . . .

JEANINE: He personally has not armed anybody . . .

FELIX, *composure rattling:* Now look, dear . . .

JEANINE: Don't call me dear! —Why can't you make that announcement?

FELIX: They have tons of hidden arms, goddamit!

EMILY, *to Felix:* Don't, darling, please . . .

FELIX, *to Emily, indignantly:* No! I can't pretend I am dealing with Jesus Christ here! I'm trying my best but the man is not just a hippie, he's also a guerilla . . . !

EMILY, *patting his head:* And he has also managed to walk through your prison wall.

FELIX: So what?—am I supposed to have an explanation for everything?

HENRI: Felix, listen; if you announce that he is no longer a wanted man you take the moral high ground, and if . . .

FELIX: Do we have laws or not? There's a homicide sentence on the man! In return for what am I lifting his sentence? *His anger returning.* I am not turning this government into a farce! I'm asking you, will he promise to keep the peace?—

JEANINE: But shouldn't you promise first? You have the tanks.

FELIX: Yes, I have the tanks and he doesn't, so he's the one who has to make the promises!

JEANINE: Well now! —So much for all this high spiritual change you've gone through . . .

HENRI: I have an idea; for just this moment, right now, try to think of this problem as though you did not have a gun.

FELIX: Right. Okay, I'm ready! You want me to talk?—here I am. *To Jeanine:* So where is he? *Slaps his hips.* No guns! I'm all ears! Where's god?

Stanley enters.

JEANINE: Stanley!

Stanley comes and embraces her.

STANLEY: How you doin', Jeanie, you're lookin' good.

JEANINE: Is . . . everything all right?

FELIX: Have you spoken with him?

STANLEY: . . . Here's the thing.

Pause.

What it all comes down to is—he's having big trouble making up his mind.

HENRI: About . . . ?

STANLEY: Getting crucified.

FELIX: What's his problem?

STANLEY: Well . . . if he doesn't, will people feel he's let them down?

JEANINE: I'm surprised at you, Stanley; his deciding to be crucified is not going to depend on whether he's disappointing people's expectations!

STANLEY: He is serious about changing the world, Jeanie, everything he does he's got to think of the effect on people. What's wrong with that?

JEANINE: What's wrong is that it changes him into one more shitty politician! Whatever he does he'll do because it's right, not to get people's approval!

FELIX: So where does that leave matters? *Violently.* . . . And try not to use so many words, will you?

STANLEY: My candid, rock bottom opinion?

FELIX: What.

STANLEY: Ignore him.

HENRI: Brilliant.

FELIX: I can't ignore him, he's broken the law, he's . . .

STANLEY: General, I don't have to tell you, even now up in the villages the crime rate's been dropping since he showed up, people are getting ready for heaven, right? A lot of them like starting to boil the water, right? And much less garbage in the street and whitewashing their houses and brushing their teeth—and the number screwing their daughters is like way down, you know. —In other words, this is a very good thing he got going for you, so how about just turning your attention . . . elsewhere?

HENRI: Brilliant. Absolutely brilliant.

FELIX: And will he "turn his attention elsewhere"? His people will go right on agitating against me, won't they. As though I had nothing to do but go around murdering people; as though I'd done nothing to improve the country, as though the British are not building two hotels, and the Dutch and Japanese weren't starting to talk to us. . . . What the hell more does he want of me!

STANLEY: Well for one thing . . . I don't know like maybe let's say, if you like stopped—you know, like knocking off union organizers . . .

FELIX: I have no outstanding orders against organizers!

JEANINE: Of course not, they're all dead.

FELIX: I'm sorry, decent people don't join unions!

EMILY: I'm in a union.

FELIX: *You!*

EMILY, *smoothing his cheek:* Don't take it to heart, dear, it's only the Directors Guild of America.

FELIX: I can't believe this, Emily . . . *you* are in a *union?*

EMILY: Felix dear, you really do have to start thinking differently . . .

FELIX, *furious:* How can I think differently if nobody else is thinking differently? —So where are we, Stanley—the war goes on? Yes or no?

STANLEY: . . . Could I please ask a favor, General? Would you leave us alone for a couple minutes?

FELIX: No! We've got to settle this!

STANLEY: I can't talk to her otherwise, okay?

EMILY: There's nothing to lose, dear. *Holding out her hand to him.* Come. Let's both have a glass of water.

FELIX, *hesitates:* . . . But I hope we understand each other.

STANLEY: We do, sir, just give me five.

EMILY: Come, Felix dear.

FELIX, *sotto, as she leads him off:* I don't know why everybody's being so fucking stupid!

> *Felix and Emily leave.*
> *Henri starts to move.*

STANLEY: You can stay if you want—it's just I didn't want to say it in front of him but in my personal opinion this thing is getting pretty nasty out there—

JEANINE: Nasty how?

STANLEY: A lot of the folks—they don't say it out loud, but they're hoping their village will be picked.

JEANINE: Picked?

STANLEY: For the crucifixion.

HENRI, *grips his head:* Oh my god!—why!

STANLEY: Well—like you know the honor of it and . . . well, the ah . . . property values.

JEANINE: *Property* values!

STANLEY: Well, face it, once it's televised they'll be jamming in from the whole entire world to see where it happened. Tour buses bumper to bumper across the Andes to get to see his bloody drawers? Buy a souvenir fingernail, T-shirts, or one of his balls? It's a whole tax base thing, Jeanie, y'know? Like maybe a new school, roads, swimming pool, maybe even a casino and theme park—all that shit. I don't have to tell you, baby, these people have *nothing*.

HENRI: We are living in hell.

STANLEY: Well yes and no; I think he figures it could also like give people some kind of hope for themselves.

JEANINE, *incredulously: Hope?* From seeing a man crucified?!

STANLEY: From seeing somebody who means it when he says he loves them, honey. So that's why—at least when I left him—he's like thinking death.

JEANINE, *bursts into tears:* Oh god . . .

STANLEY: —So what I'm hoping . . . can I tell you? —Cause you're the only one he'd possibly listen to . . . I guess because you tried to die yourself.

Jeanine lifts her eyes to him.

STANLEY: . . . I really wish you'd tell him he's got to live . . . and just maybe forget about . . . you know, being god. I mean even if he is.

Jeanine moans in pain.

We've got to face it, Jeanie, in a couple weeks people forget, you know? Nothing much lasts anymore, and if they nail him up it's eventually blow away like everything else. I mean he's just got to . . .

JEANINE: . . . Give up his glory.

STANLEY: Maybe not quite—he's already waked up a lot of people that things don't have to be this way. He could settle for that. —You're the only one who could save him, Jeanie. Please, for all of us. Make him live.

HENRI: And of course, to return to basics, we still don't know for sure . . . who and what he really is, do we.

Pause.

JEANINE: Do we know, Stanley? Tell me the truth.

STANLEY: Oh, Jeanie, I wish I knew! Some days it's like he walked straight out of the ocean or a cloud or a bush full of roses. Other days . . . Shrugs. . . . he smells a lot like anybody else.

JEANINE: Then what do you want me to say to him, exactly?

STANLEY: . . . I think he has to . . . well . . . agree to a deal that if Felix will stop persecuting people he'll . . . you know . . . disappear.

JEANINE: Forever?

STANLEY: Well . . . I guess so . . . yeah.

JEANINE: I'm to ask him not to be god.

STANLEY: No—no, he could be god like . . . in a more general inspirational way. I mean the actual improvements would just have to be up to us, that's all.

HENRI: Wonderful! He's still god but he goes away and there's no bloodbath! Peace!

JEANINE: And each for himself.

HENRI: Peace! Or the country is done, finished, a heap of bones!

Long pause.

JEANINE, *to Stanley:* All right, I want him alive. We haven't the greatness to deserve his death. —I just hope I never hear that he's mowing the lawn.

STANLEY: Nobody's pure, baby—if that's what's bothering you . . .

JEANINE: So if he comes again. . . . Tell me what to say.

STANLEY: . . . Just say . . . like—"Charley darling . . ."

JEANINE: Charley?

STANLEY: He changed it last night. Said it was really Charley from now on, not Jack. Although he's changed it on me a dozen times. Vladimir once, Francisco . . . Herby for a week or two . . . Just say, like . . .

The light comes on, but dimly. He looks about. A music very distant, subliminal.

STANLEY: Charley? Is that you?

The light brightens sharply. All straighten, look slightly upward.

Felix enters with Emily.

FELIX, *feeling the air:* Something is happening . . . !

STANLEY: Ssh—please!

FELIX: Who are you telling to sshh!

EMILY, *end of her patience:* For god's sake, will you control yourself! *To Stanley, pointing up to the light:* Is that . . . ?

STANLEY: I think so.

JEANINE, *facing upward:* How I love you, darling. Now please, please listen to me!

FELIX, *looking about combatively:* Well where is he, goddamit!

EMILY, *pointing up:* The light, dear, the light!

FELIX, *realizing now, looking up with dawning fear:* Holy shi . . .

STANLEY, *upward:* I've got an idea, baby, if you'd like to consider it.

JEANINE: Whatever you decide you are my life and my hope, darling.

STANLEY: You've like turned the country inside out, you know? There's lots of changes since you showed up . . . compared, you know? So maybe, just as—you know, a suggestion—we're thinking maybe the best thing right now, would be for you to . . . just let it hang the way it is. Stand pat. Don't make your move, you know? Bleiben sie ruhig, baby; vaya con calme; ne t'en fais pas; spokoine-e gospodin; nin bu yao jaoji—dig?

> *As Skip, the two soldiers, and the crew all appear, looking up and about.*

SKIP: We've got thirty-five minutes of sun . . . where is he?

FELIX, *finger raised:* Ssh—that's him!

SKIP, *looking up: What's him?*

JEANINE, *to the air:* Adore you, darling.

FELIX, *to Stanley:* Are you talking to him or not?

STANLEY: I'm not sure, I think so.

FELIX: Tell him I'll call off the search and we can forget the whole thing if he goes away and never comes back!

SKIP: Goes away!—we have a contract, sir!

JEANINE, *furious:* And empty the jails, of course. And the torturers are to be prosecuted!

FELIX: What torturers?

JEANINE, *to Heaven:* Come down, Charley!

FELIX, *to Heaven:* Wait!! Hold it! —Okay, you stay up there indefinitely, and I'll . . . fire the torturers.

SKIP: This is a contractual breach!—he's got to come down!

FELIX, *to Skip, retrieving authority:* . . . Will you shut up? I've still got him under arrest, don't I?!

STANLEY: . . . That's about it, Charley, okay? I mean we're going to miss you, baby, especially those fantastic conversations on the beach, but . . . you know, maybe it's all for the best, right? I mean, could you give us a sign?

Maybe you tell him, Jeanie, could you?

JEANINE: Oh my dear, my darling, it cuts my heart to say this but I think maybe you better not come back! I'm going to miss you terribly, nothing will be the same . . . but I guess you really have to go!

STANLEY: I'm not trying to rush you, baby, but can we have some kind of an answer?

SKIP: Just a minute, I'd like a word with him. *Comes down, center—sotto:* What's his latest name again?

STANLEY: Charley.

SKIP, *looking up:* Charles? You simply have to return, there's no question about it. I will only remind you that my agency has a signed contract with this government to televise your crucifixion and we have paid a substantial sum of money for the rights. I will forebear mentioning our stockholders, many of them widows and aged persons, who have in good faith bought shares in our company. I plead with you as a responsible, feeling person—show yourself and serve your legal sentence. I want to assure you that everyone from the top of my company to the bottom will be everlastingly grateful and will mourn your passing all the days of our lives. —A practical note: the sun is rapidly going down so may I have the favor of a quick reply? Thank you very much.

All look about expectantly, but nothing happens.

FELIX, *stepping up to the center:* Now listen, Charley, I'm having some second thoughts about this deal I mentioned—you just have to come down and get crucified.

JEANINE: You just promised not to . . . !

FELIX: The country's desperate! If he stays up there I will have to return some of the money!

SKIP: All of it, General.

FELIX: Well, we'll discuss that.

JEANINE: So much for your word!

FELIX, *to Jeanine:* That money will mean hundreds of jobs . . . ! *Upward:* I'm planning on school upgrading, health clinics, lots of improvements for the folks. Whereas if I have to return some of the money . . .

SKIP: All of it!

FELIX: I am not returning that goddam money!

Emily steps up.

EMILY: May I, Skip?

Skip steps aside, gesturing to her to move in. She looks up.

I'm afraid I have to differ with my friend Skip, and my dear friend General Barriaux. —Wherever you are, Charley, I beg you stay there.

FELIX: This is terrible stuff you're telling the man! You are condemning this country to ruin!

EMILY, *persisting to the light:* Don't make me photograph you hanging from two sticks, I beg you, Charley! Stay where you are and you will live in all our imaginations where the great images never die. Wish you all the best, my dear . . . be well!

FELIX, *to the light:* All right now, just listen to me . . .

HENRI, *to the light:* Whoever you are!—I thank you for my daughter's return to life. And before your loving heart I apologize for ignoring her for so many years, and for having led her in my blind pride to the brink of destruction.

PHIL: Speaking for the crew—*Sees Skip react.* . . . this is not a strike! *To the light:* But we'd appreciate it a lot if you, you know, just didn't show. . . . *Sees Skip react.* We're ready to go as the contract calls for! But . . . *Upward:* well, that's the message.

SKIP, *upward:* Now look here, Charles —we have fifteen minutes of sun . . . !

> *He is stopped by the low, rumbling bass of a great organ heard as from a distance.*

STANLEY: Sshh! *He looks around for the source of the sound—the others too. Then upward again:* Am I hearing the ocean in the background, Charley? I visualize you on the beach, right? Staring out at the sea, making up your mind? —Let me say one more final thing, okay?—the country's like nice and quiet at least for the moment, right?—give or take a minor ambush here and there? After thirty-eight years of killing, so they tell me, it's almost normal now, right? —So the thing is, Charley—do you want to light the match that'll explode the whole place again?

FELIX: Don't worry about the country, Charley, I'll take care of it. You come down, you hear me? I'm talking syndication, this is one big pot of money! I'm talking new hotels, I'm talking new construction, I'm talking investment. You care about people? Come down and get crucified!

JEANINE, *starting to weep:* For all our sakes, my darling, don't come down . . . !

SKIP AND FELIX, *upward:* You can't do this to us!

They look about, wait . . . then . . .

SKIP, *to Felix:* You will return that check, or I'm calling the Embassy!

FELIX: Fuck the Embassy, I'm keeping the money . . . !

They continue shouting at each other, vanishing into the crowd . . .

SKIP: This is larceny! I'll call Washington! You are destroying my career!

FELIX: I did my good-faith best!

STANLEY: Go away, Charley, before they all kill each other! You gotta give us a sign, baby, what's it gonna be!

The light slowly fades to black, as they all look upward and about in wonder and apprehension.

STANLEY, *in the silence, tentatively:* Charley?

All wait, all glancing about. Nothing happens.

We're not seeing the light, okay?

Silence; all listening.

Don't hear the ocean, okay?

Silence . . . then . . .

They are weeping, immensely relieved and sorry.

HENRI: Good-bye, Charley.

EMILY: Good-bye, Charley.

FELIX: Good-bye, Charley.

SARAH: Good-bye, Charley.

PHIL: Good-bye, Charley.

Skip turns and angrily walks out.

JEANINE: Good-bye, my darling! . . . But could you think about . . . maybe trying it . . . another time?

> *Silence. Henri takes Jeanine's arm and they move; each of the others now leave the stage silently, in various directions, each alone.*

STANLEY, *lifts a hand in farewell, looking forward and up:* Always love you, baby. And look, if you ever feel like, you know . . . a cup of tea, or a glass of dry white, don't hesitate, okay? . . . I'm always home. *Salutes.* Thanks.

> *He walks off alone.*

End.

FOR THE BEST IN PAPERBACKS, LOOK FOR THE

In every corner of the world, on every subject under the sun, Penguin represents quality and variety—the very best in publishing today.

For complete information about books available from Penguin—including Penguin Classics, Penguin Compass, and Puffins—and how to order them, write to us at the appropriate address below. Please note that for copyright reasons the selection of books varies from country to country.

In the United States: Please write to *Penguin Group (USA), P.O. Box 12289 Dept. B, Newark, New Jersey 07101-5289* or call 1-800-788-6262.

In the United Kingdom: Please write to *Dept. EP, Penguin Books Ltd, Bath Road, Harmondsworth, West Drayton, Middlesex UB7 0DA.*

In Canada: Please write to *Penguin Books Canada Ltd, 90 Eglinton Avenue East, Suite 700, Toronto, Ontario M4P 2Y3.*

In Australia: Please write to *Penguin Books Australia Ltd, P.O. Box 257, Ringwood, Victoria 3134.*

In New Zealand: Please write to *Penguin Books (NZ) Ltd, Private Bag 102902, North Shore Mail Centre, Auckland 10.*

In India: Please write to *Penguin Books India Pvt Ltd, 11 Panchsheel Shopping Centre, Panchsheel Park, New Delhi 110 017.*

In the Netherlands: Please write to *Penguin Books Netherlands bv, Postbus 3507, NL-1001 AH Amsterdam.*

In Germany: Please write to *Penguin Books Deutschland GmbH, Metzlerstrasse 26, 60594 Frankfurt am Main.*

In Spain: Please write to *Penguin Books S. A., Bravo Murillo 19, 1° B, 28015 Madrid.*

In Italy: Please write to *Penguin Italia s.r.l., Via Benedetto Croce 2, 20094 Corsico, Milano.*

In France: Please write to *Penguin France, Le Carré Wilson, 62 rue Benjamin Baillaud, 31500 Toulouse.*

In Japan: Please write to *Penguin Books Japan Ltd, Kaneko Building, 2-3-25 Koraku, Bunkyo-Ku, Tokyo 112.*

In South Africa: Please write to *Penguin Books South Africa (Pty) Ltd, Private Bag X14, Parkview, 2122 Johannesburg.*